Expression

Consciousness

Spencer David

Expression of Consciousness

Spencer David

Cover: Lee-Anne Higgs

Voice of Spirit Publishers
2019

First Printing 2019

ISBN: 978-1-5272-4482-5 (Paperback)

Voice of Spirit Publishers
Coventry, United Kingdom

Website: www.expressionofconsciousness.co.uk

Ordering Information:

Special discounts are available on quantity purchases by corporations, associations, educators, and others. For details, contact the publisher using the above details.

This book is dedicated to my dear friend Paul Hogan.

Deeply Missed. Never Forgotten. Always Loved.
Rest In Peace.

Contents

Introduction

The purpose of writing this book, is to aid those that have just started their spiritual journey, and for those that may have been on theirs for some time. The aim is to bring understanding of truth through my experiences from the world of spirit, and what the universe has taught me to be truth, from a point of awareness whilst writing this book.

I first began to write this book back in 2004, at first it flowed quite well over a couple of weeks or months then it became much harder to write. I suddenly realised there was nothing to write, and because I could not describe what was truly going on from my level of understanding as it was all very new to me.

I was trying to write about something I had not fully understood myself, and I am still continuing to learn something new every day. 15 years later now in 2019 with around 20 years of experience, self-development, sitting in circles, researching, running my own circles, workshops, private readings and platform work, I feel its time to accomplish my goal.

The information in this book should draw your awareness to the truth that we are all one, we are all relative, and we are all connected to consciousness; The life source.

Consciousness is the intangible force behind everything, everything has purpose, and without

Consciousness there would not be 'LIFE', there would not be existence at all.

Reading this book will hopefully convey you to a point of awareness that will show you, that you are more valuable than you may currently realise at this present time.

Through my personal experiences, it has aided me to grow and understand what being "spiritual" truly means to me.

By the end of the book it should allow you to see you are not just a human being, but a sentient being, a multi-dimensional being a multi-conscious being, you will gather an understand that everything is about Energy and Frequency.

"If you want to find the secrets of the universe,
Think in terms of energy,
Frequency and Vibration"

Nikola Tesla.

A Medium does not stop the grieving, but eases the pain.
This was given to me by my own spirit guide Running Deer in
2004.

Enjoy...

Chapter 1
Where it all Began

I grew up in Coventry from a working class background; my parents had their own second hand furniture shop and sold a variety of items.

My family were not overly religious although I vaguely remember attending Sunday school a couple of times as a child.

I do recall it was at that present time, talking to me about the existence of God and religion was not of any interest to me, as I was a child and having fun was more entertaining, like all children.

Growing up I have no recollection of making contact with the spirit world, not until my adult life after a conversations with my mother and a close friend Marie I used to work with.

My mum was a believer of the afterlife/the Spirit World, which again was only something I found out about in my young adult life.

I was well aware that she read horror books and read stories about hauntings, my mother also had the series of books by Doris Stokes, which I am very grateful to now have. We never spoke about what my mum believed in, until I started my own spiritual path at the age of 21. My mum had spoken about her mother at times and told us she was a Catholic, my grandmother sadly passed away when my mum was 10yrs old so I never got to meet her.

In actual fact I never met any of my grandparents like my brother and two sisters did, so when growing up and stories were shared, I couldn't really relate to them, because those they were talking about were total strangers to me, so to speak.

My mother believed in spiritualism for all, or for most of her life. She had told me in the past about visions she had, she never developed it, but did attend Spiritualist Churches and kept it very quiet because it scared my dad. My mum got to see the late and highly respected evidential medium Doris Stokes a couple of times over the years too.

My mother did not get a message from Doris, but her best friend did. Doris told my mums friend about the 7 babies she tragically lost over a period of time all by miscarriage. This information was brought through by her daughter, whom heartbreakingly, had passed in a car accident in Spain, years previous due to her flip flop becoming stuck under the brake pedal, driving through mountain roads which Doris confirmed as a way of her evidence.

I remember a couple of stories she told me about as regards to her visions. On one occasion whilst on holiday with my father, my mum had a dream about two local boys who were involved in an accident. The two boys were riding their bikes near a cliff edge near the sea. As the boys were out riding, my mum explained to me she saw one of the boys lose control of his push bike, failing to brake and the boy slipping off the cliff taking his bike with him and unfortunately died from the fall.

My mum continued with the story of her vision and went on to say what happened next. When my mum and dad woke she discussed the dream with my dad, according to my mum my dad said It's a dream, there is nothing to worry about" so they continued with the day. Whilst they were both out, my mum told me that they walked past a shop, and my mum noticed the newspapers.

She told me that she picked up a newspaper, and the front page had the story about the two boys on a bike ride and confirming everything in her vision to be true. This did freak my dad out and as a result he stopped my mum going to the spiritual churches because he said it "was bringing in bad energy"

On another occasion she said she had a vision about a very large fish tank we had in our house before I was born. My mother told me whilst she was out she had a vision of the fish tank breaking in the living room. When my mum returned home the fish tank was broken and the fish were found on the living room floor, the living room flooded and the fish couldn't be saved sadly.

My mother became a huge support to me throughout my spiritual path, and managed to see me achieve a lot of my goals, leading up until she passed in September 2011. My mum took me to see many of the local spiritual churches around Coventry and we enjoyed watching many talented mediums, we received many messages over the years.

Going to the various churches and sitting within the congregation, gave me the opportunity to watch and study the presentation and delivery of prayer, philosophy and evidential messages from peoples loved ones in spirit. So how did I get to that point, going to the spiritual churches with my mum?

I was with a friend called Andy and we went to our local mini market, this was where we knew another friend that worked there called Jav, he worked at the shop that was a family run business. We all knew each other for a few years and there were many occasions where I spent a few hours with Jav to keep him company and sometimes help out.

On this particular evening as I was just entering the door of the shop with Andy and Jav asked me if I had heard the news about our friend Paul. "No" I replied, "Why what's happened now?" With a bit of a giggle in my voice, because I started to think Paul may have had a stupid accident at work like dropping a brick on his foot because he was a brick hod carrier.

Jav quickly responded back "He's committed suicide mate." I replied back sharply "F**k Off, that's not even funny Jav!!" I continued to say to him "I never heard that, I'm going back outside, and I'm going to walk back in, and you are going to change the subject!" I walked out, and then back in like nothing had happened, and I heard the same news again, "Spence he has done it, he took his own life last night mate."

From this point I don't recall what was said or happened for a couple of minutes, the shock made my mind instantly shut down, people where talking, but all I heard was silence, my body just went totally numb, I couldn't tell you what was going on in my head, it was like it was going on all around me, and I wasn't "there".

I remember after maybe two or three minutes where my mind began to absorb what Andy and Jav where talking about, for a couple of moments I just kept hearing, "Spence you okay?" as I'm standing in the doorway staring vacantly at the floor, totally dumbstruck scratching my head. Your mind goes into overload with thoughts trying to address and calculate if what you just heard was true. NO, NO, NO I'm thinking, it can't be?

I then walked out of the shop, sat on a wall close by, trying to register what the hell had happened, another local friend called Ellie who is very bubbly, loud, but has been a good friend since we were around 10 years old, and we're still friends. She was crossing the road towards me "Hiiiiiiiii" Ellie shouted, unfortunately for her she was unaware of the last 5 or so minutes that had just occurred, and I just started screaming profanities at the top of my voice at her and making no sense at all.

That evening I spent the next 3 hours walking the streets, with Andy, and not a single word was said.
Paul was 4 years older than me, and on many occasions he socialised with Jav a couple of other friends and I at the shop.
Paul was into body building and if he wasn't working as a brick hod carrier, he would be in his local gym lifting weights that I would need a forklift for.

He was around 6.2 ft. tall, of a large build with the kindest of hearts and personalities. He wasn't somebody that looked for trouble, a few days after hearing about his suicide it became knowledge to us that Paul struggled with the loss of his mother, and a couple of other things that had gone on within his private life. He was a very private person in all and kept a lot from us because from what I understand now, he wasn't the talking type about certain things.

Over the next couple of years I went to college and then University, I was also a youth worker at President Kennedy School, which I started as a volunteer with disabled young adults.

My job in youth work came about because I was registered partially sighted when I was 16 and had support for my sight through my school years. My mum found out about the disabled youth club when I was 16 years old which I attended there for around 6 months.

The staff had been watching me over the past months and monitoring my relations with the other members of the youth club. On a particular week attending the group a member of staff asked to speak to me privately in the office, so I went in and sat down the senior youth club staff member started talking to me about my connection with the other members, and she was pleased to watch how I interacted and supported the other disabled members.

When they struggled with things such as playing table tennis or pool, I would offer support and help to try and teach them a way of making things easier for them. During the time I was at President Kennedy

School I competed at trampolining for numerous years for them.

Due to my experience in trampolining I could also be a teaching assistant, of which became very resourceful for the disabled youth club as it meant I could work alongside qualified teachers until I was put on a teachers training course myself.

During the meeting the senior staff explained that there was an opportunity of a volunteer position as a member of staff at the disabled youth club, I accepted without hesitation.

Around 12 months later, the youth service employed me and this led me to meeting another important person in my life called Marie who I worked alongside with another girl called Elaine for a couple of years, and it was Marie that assisted the beginning of my spiritual journey.

One Friday night I went out for social drinks with Elaine and Marie, after a couple of drinks we started talking about haunted places, ghosts and Ouija boards, the whole spooky thing. At this point in my life I didn't believe in life after death, but I did have an interest in the paranormal and ghosts thanks to my mother.

I did read things about poltergeists and stuff and people claiming they had seen things in their house move on their own, even whilst reading this kind of thing I still wasn't 100% sure that these claims where true, if it was true, then why had I not seen it?

My friend Marie started talking about people having visions and being able to contact deceased loved ones.

She was also talking about some of her childhood, saying she had invisible friends or "Spirit friends". Marie explained at times she suffered from a lot of headaches caused by the pressure from spirits that where trying to make contact with her on a regular basis.

Now to me this was something completely different and on the next level, and way over my head. I looked at my other friend Elaine and she looked more unconvinced than I did. I mean, at least I thought there might be "something out there" but Elaine was having none of it, as far as she was concerned it was all nonsense.

As for me, in the back of my mind I was thinking "What if?" and "Where are all these deceased loved ones?" and "What do they do wherever they are?" At this stage Marie continues talking about these visions and says she has the ability to "see" things before they happen. Well when Marie told us she could do this I was like, this girl is one flew over the cuckoo's nest!

Marie focuses her attention to me about Paul, my friend who took his own life 4 years previous and suggested maybe I should go and see a medium. Marie explained why she wanted me to go, to try and help me deal with the loss of Paul.

Marie and Elaine were all too familiar how I was dealing with Paul, and at the time I wasn't dealing with it very well at all. Yes I was studying at University at the time and working, but only a small handful knew I was blocking the passing of Paul out, well at least trying to with drink and smoking Cannabis, and we all know that doesn't work, because it didn't.

When I was smoking cannabis it may have relaxed me, but it wasn't enough so I drank with it. I need to point out I wasn't doing this daily, because I was at Uni and working, so I would have blow-outs, or stop at friend's house or flat at weekends or certain evenings if I didn't have to go to university the next morning.

Marie continued to explain what mediums do, and hearing a message from Paul maybe something I need to hear, and she mentioned a local spiritualist church was holding a psychic supper the following weekend, so I agreed to go.

The evening drew to a close, and we walked home still talking of the main subject of the night, as we were walking home the only thing I was worried about now was I hope I don't get nightmares because to be honest I can get easily scared. When I watch horror films I am the first person to dive under the pillow when something scary happens, now I can't watch them at all, because of the intention and energy behind them, I also have a tendency to cry at films too.

When I got home I was quite baffled about what we were talking about, but one thing was for sure I needed to find out the answers to my questions. Is there life after death? Can people contact the dead? Or Can the dead contact the living? Can people really see spirits? I don't remember having invisible spirit friends when I was young, and at this point I wasn't aware what my mum was going to tell me in a couple of weeks' time.

I decided to make arrangements to meet Marie around her house one-day when we were not working and talk about mediums and spirit in a bit more detail. We sat down with a glass of orange juice and Marie started talking about her spirit friends and experiences, plus more information about what mediums do.

We discussed about the spiritualist church, and suggested I should go and see what I think of it. Marie said there are mediums there who can contact passed over loved ones, and she started talking about their abilities and different methods of making contact with spirit using Clairvoyance, Clairsentience and Clairaudience. The ability to see spirit is called Clairvoyance, to sense spirit it's called Clairsentience and lastly to hear spirit it's called Clairaudience.

By now I was very fascinated by all this, so I asked her if it would it be possible to get hold of a dearly missed friend who committed suicide in 1995. I have to admit at this point he had been passed over around 5 years and I was still grieving for my friend.

Marie had been to the cemetery with me a few times and I frequently told her how much I missed him, and needed reassurance that he was ok. She said to me that we can arrange to go to the psychic Supper at the spiritual church that she went to. I was told a medium might give a message to me from him, if it's meant to be.

I went home that day excited and nervous about this new chapter in my life I was about to experience. I told my mum straight away about what Marie and I discussed, "and we are going to see a medium." My mums' response was "Go, there is nothing to worry about." My mother said encouragingly.

This is when I became more aware about my mums abilities and her connection with Spiritualist Churches, and also getting in touch with her mother. I thought well there is only one way to find out, and that's to go and see for myself.

My mother also said that there may be a chance I will get a message from my Grandmother and Grandfather. I thought getting messages from my grandparents would be a little strange because like I have mentioned previously unfortunately all my grandparents passed over before I was born.

Chapter 2
Hearing from Them for the First Time

The day came when Marie, her sister and I went to the church, for the medium Psychic Supper. It was a wet and dull day in November, and not too warm.

When I got inside the church it wasn't anything like I expected. I was expecting to see Jesus on the cross everywhere like other churches, but it looked more like an ordinary hall. If I remember rightly there were about ten tables in the room and about six people to a table, and a chair for the mediums. We chose a table and sat down, I was nervously looking around the room trying to figure out who the mediums where.

The mediums were called out to join those of us in the main hall, a lady sat at our table, there was an open prayer first from another medium in the room, then my waiting came to an end, she introduced herself and immediately said "Can I come to you sir?" meaning me.

"Yes" I said, looking around our table still nervous.

The lady began relaying information to me.

"I have a lady here, saying she is your grandmother, on your mothers' side." She continued "this lady is of a small build, around 4ft 9 inches tall, she had a breathing condition prior to her passing, and I believe it to be TB, and she is coming though with lots of love and support for you."

I had to wait to get this information confirmed when I got home, because there was lots of information about my grandparents I didn't know about.

She continued talking about my grandparents for a few minutes, and I felt fine with it. The medium then brought my mums dad through, and the medium started talking about my struggled road, without giving much away to the others on the table I was sitting at.

My grandfather on my mothers' side of the family, gave me confirmation that he had been watching me over the past few years, and told me to stay focused, and I would also need to make some large decisions regarding my own future.

Suddenly she proclaimed "I have a tall young man with me; I would say he is in his late teens or early twenties. He is built like a" and paused, I knew what she meant. All of a sudden I knew where she was going with this.

"He is making me aware, that he took his own life, do you understand this young man?" I replied "Yes" with a crokey voice, as I had to clear my throat at the same time, as emotion within me started to surface.

"He is saying he past to the world of spirit rather quickly, and his name is Paul."

Now she had my full attention, apart from the fact my mind was asking itself how on earth she knew Paul! I had never met this woman in my life and she is talking about my friend who committed suicide.
"He is saying you have a good future ahead of you, but you're at a bit of a cross roads"
I looked at her in astonishment "Yes."
"I am feeling a bit low and things are not going to well at the moment." I said.

She stated to me, "Well he is saying you are going to be fine, don't waste your life like he did, he is watching over you." She continued "He is saying he is sorry for what he has done, but now he is fine and is now in a better place with his mother."
Now I was starting to realise she was talking to Paul.
I knew one of the reasons Paul took his own life was because he couldn't get over the death of his mother, like I previously mentioned.

I found out Paul and his mother were very close, he didn't speak about it, if Paul had a problem he was the one that wouldn't say much about the problems he was having. "He is asking you to pass his love on to his family, will you do this?"
"I will try, I don't know where his father is at the moment but I will do my best." I replied.   This is because I lost touch with the family.
"I will leave his love with you, god bless." She said and moved on to another person.

As she moved on to the next person, I was deeply in thought about 5 minutes of my life. I don't know how many times I asked myself 'Did that just happen?'

I was completely confused and stunned with the whole thing.

Marie asked if I was ok.

Sounding quite distant I replied "Yeah"

I did feel really strange, I would try and describe it, but I'm afraid I can't. I'm sure you know what I mean though.

At this point I needed some air and a fag to try and get my head sort of round what had just happened.

I went outside scratching my head whilst I walked out of the doors. I don't know why but for some reason I actually enjoyed that cigarette.

I was still asking myself "what just happened in there?" but I couldn't get any answers. After a few minutes alone with myself something was telling me inside that Paul made contact.

At the time I didn't know why I knew, but I knew, I eventually went back inside and enjoyed the rest of the afternoon, the mediums had finished the readings, so this gave people a chance to talk amongst themselves about their messages whilst eating our meals. When I got home I told my mum what had happened and she was very supportive.

While I was sitting at home thinking about the day's events, it did bring a few tears to my eyes. To be fair the reading was just what I needed to help my grieving, at the time it didn't remove the grieving completely but it had eased it a little.

For a couple of years after Paul passed, I could not go out with friends and not think about him without getting upset. This is also the first time I have wrote down my feelings for Paul, and I still get a lump in my throat, even now while I am writing this. I can say though, when I have readings from mediums, I do feel uplifted when he comes across through to talk to me because now I know and understand he is helping me on the other side.

So a few days later I went to Marie's house to talk about the Psychic Supper.
I told her I was very convinced there was life on the other side, I wanted to indulge further into spiritualism but didn't know where to start. Marie suggested I go back to the church with her and see what I think about the open circle sessions.

This is where anyone of all backgrounds can find out if they can contact the spirit world for themselves and pass on messages to others in the room; the purpose of open circles is also to help you to become spiritually aware, and to connect with our inner knowledge.
After a long discussion about various things, I decided to go.

It was half term so Marie and I didn't have to attend work at our local school, at the youth club we worked at, so our evening was free.
We also went along with another mutual friend called Anthony, we got to the church about 7.15pm and there were approximately fifteen other people in the group and 2 mediums running it, we got ourselves a glass of water and sat in the circle.
I was very nervous at this point and did not know what to expect, but I knew I wasn't going to see or talk to any spirits... well; at least that's what I thought!

One of the mediums asked the group if anyone had not been before and I cowardly put up my hand. He continued and explained there was nothing to worry about and I was quite safe and protected in the church. Quite safe! Protected! I thought, Marie never told me this was dangerous!

The group was then told to relax, close our eyes, calm the mind and just focus upon our breathing for a few moments, before they assist us all through a guided meditation.

I began to closed my eyes and started to become quite relaxed, the room went all quiet accept for the voice of the medium who was doing the guided meditation. The medium continued with the meditation and his guidance started to begin.

We were told to see within our mind's eye a path and envision ourselves walking forwards, following the pathway ahead. The medium continued "As you follow this path, you will become more relaxed and at peace within yourself, and that calming energy will gently flow through you" he went on to say "Within the distance you will start to see a staircase, this staircase has seven steps and you will climb these steps one at a time"

I was focusing and I was completely engulfed with the feeling of peace all around my being, I could feel it gently flow around and through me, like gentle waves of water floating in to shore, and gracefully washing over the sandy bed.

I commenced to the staircase, and slowly in my mind I could visualise the entrance to the stairwell, so I preceded forwards and could still hear the gentle voice of the medium, instructing us to go the stairs and take each step one at a time.

At this point as I was approaching the stairs, I began to feel much lighter; there was no feeling of physical density or limitation, like the physical world.

It was a sense of tranquillity like I had never felt before, although I was having this amazing euphoric feeling, still within the constructs of my own mind, I could not help thinking to myself what is at the top of the stairs, or who?

Although I was not sure who was going to meet me at the top, I had no sense of fear even though I had never done this before and had no idea of what to expect, but it was so comforting, and strong reassuring feeling, a new feeling of awareness, of complete bliss.

Whilst the medium explained the next phase of the meditation "When you get to the top step there will be a door, and behind the door you will enter a library of spiritual knowledge" he went on to say "have a look around this room filled with books, from ceiling to floor, wall to wall"

I finally made it to the top of the stairs, as I entered the library it was like he said it would be, floor to ceiling, and all walls covered with shelves full of books of all sizes.

The shelves were crafted out of the finest of wood and the image in my 'minds' eye was so vibrant and full of colour. The colours were far more radiant than the human eye could see, it was a place that felt so familiar, but I had not been there before, but it felt like I knew the place.

"There will be a bookcase in this room, take a book that you are drawn to." The medium told us, I wasn't

"Drawn" to any book I was just still sitting there, but I did see the bookcase.

"You may be greeted by a loved one from spirit, they maybe a loved one of your own, or for someone else within the group, and they may want to talk to you."

The medium continued to say "If they contact you please remember what they say, to pass a message on to someone in the room."

I was still looking around the library in my 'minds' view, taking in as much of the experience as I possibly could; all of a sudden I started to see thin beans of light with the colours of blue, silver and green. From my view point I was standing in the bottom right corner of the room, looking towards the centre. The beans of shimmering translucent light were coming from the ceiling and the floor, projecting themselves diagonally towards the centre of the room.

The rods of light joined together in the centre of the library hovering high off the floor, the radiant translucent spectrums of light became brighter and brighter and sparkling with great enthusiasm, as more and more of this light was heading to the centre of the library.

In the centre of the room the light started to take the form of an egg, glowing and shimmering continuously, with all the different colours of blue, silver and green, vibrating and pulsating outwardly.

At this point I was very unsure of what was happening but strangely I wasn't worried or frightened. I was in a state of amazement more than fear, fear was nowhere within in my mind or being, and at the time I was at total peace.

The egg shaped phenomena started to change shape again, it started to become narrower near the top of the egg, trying to form what at first I thought it would be a circle shaped top, but then formed more of a head shape.

The bottom began to move upwards, creating a split at the bottom of the egg, then very quickly it started to build more of a human shape of light, this light began to form other colours and taking the form of a gentleman. What I saw I can only describe as a hologram image in front of me, a slight transparency look to it but I could see every piece of detail on him.

Out of the blue this man appeared to which looked like to me as a grandfather figure, I could see he was about 5ft 10 inches tall with a medium build; slim, was bald on top of his head with a bit of thin hair at the sides. He was wearing dark trousers, a lemon coloured shirt and a pair of glasses. He did not move or say anything; he just stood there silently, and calmly looking into my direction.

I didn't recognise this gentleman, but he wanted to come to me for some reason. Is he for me? Is he for someone else? I was so mesmerised by what I just witness, I was too stunned to ask anything to him. He continued to stand in the centre of the room looking at me, with a gentle golden glow around him a term I would use now, is an auric field of energy which glows around the physical body.

When everybody and I came-round from the meditation the medium asked us all for feedback about what they saw. There were a few people there that where very good, for example one said to a lady "I have your mother here, I am aware she is of a small build, short in height, brown curly hair, and she would need to use a wheelchair before she passed from a stroke." After giving other pieces of evidence, the person would then relay the message from the lady's mother.

Eventually it was my turn to give some feedback on what I experienced, after I heard the things other people were giving out I thought to myself I had nothing like that, so I felt a little embarrassed and told the mediums leading the group that I saw the staircase and the library, but I held back on the other information. The medium who was running the group told me that was a successful meditation, as I managed to get something on my first time being there.

I was sitting there a little sheepish as all attention was on me, I politely thanked the medium for his feedback, everybody managed to give information of what they experienced in the circle, and the evening came to a close and finished with a prayer and everybody went home.

Marie, Anthony and I went for a drink before we went home and had a little chat about the circle.
I eventually came clean with what I saw in the church and I thought they were both going to laugh at me; Anthony didn't take what I saw too seriously, he had to make a joke out of it, which was quite normal for him. Marie on the other hand was a little more insightful on spiritualism so she came up with the idea I may be able to see spirit.

At this stage I started to make jokes myself about it then because I found it a little bit too hard to believe. I mean, the first time in a circle and I have no clue on what kind of ability I have, if I have one at all, and all of a sudden I see a spirit for the first time. In all honesty now from my understanding and of teaching myself, it is quite common for that to happen for some people.

That evening when I got home, my mum was waiting up for me to hear what happened at the open circle. As I am walking through from the kitchen to the living room I can hear my mums voice "So what happened then love?" as I entered the room, I replied "It was amazing and I saw an old man in the meditation we had to do."
"Wow" she said "Who was he?" I had sat myself down in my chair in the living room at this point and looked back at my mum to tell her what had happened. As I began to answer her I noticed she had hung a new photo on the far wall in the direction I was looking. "Where has that photo come from?" I asked. "It's a photo of your granddad I got enlarged and framed the other day." Due to my sight I previously mentioned I couldn't see it well enough, so I had to walk over to get a closer look.

I started to study the photograph on the wall further, and then I began to notice something "Oh my God!" I muttered under my breath. I continued to examine the photo and I noticed he was wearing a lemon shirt, dark trousers, and balding with hair around the side of his head, a slim build and wearing glasses. I turned back to face my mother and said "That's who I seen tonight in the meditation!" as the pitch of my voice began to rise into a squeak. "That doesn't surprise me; he spoke to you last week at the psychic supper." My mum replied. I sat back in my chair and I told my mother what happened in detail.

A few days later I had another chat to Marie and I decided to go further into it, out of curiosity more than anything to see what else may happen. I started to go regularly on Monday afternoons when I wasn't at work.

I realised it wasn't as easy as I had first thought, I didn't see any more spirits or get anything really except colours floating around in front of me, in my 'minds' eye. I told the person who was running the group what I was getting, and they told me it was 'Spiritual energy' and I got these sensations for around 18 months, before it began to develop further.

Over the next 18 months or so I started to slowly get more and more sensations and feelings and experiences in the open circle. I had feelings like tickling on my face, which many of you would have heard the term "cobwebs on the face" during your personal journey. I also started to receive feelings of people's conditions that had passed, such as a feeling of a heart attack or breathing problems. This is Clairsentience/ or Clear feeling.

I was told that the spirit world communicates with us in many different ways, and it was the start of the different ways of 'spirit' working with me. It was also explained that medium-ship development cannot be rushed, and rightly so.

I started to get shivers, cold spots around me, and generally feeling quite cold when the energy of spirit came close to me. These experiences happened during the many times I was sitting in circle and on many occasions around my home, or where ever I was at particular times.

Over time I slowly began to be able to hear the odd word or name, of which also increased to short sentences to start the process of being able to pass on messages from the loved ones in spirit, this is Clairaudience or Clear Hearing. This eventually led me at times to be able to see spirit, which is called Clairvoyance or Clear Seeing.

We can't rush or force this natural development because the human mind simply will not allow it, plus when we work with the spirit world; our experiences come from our point of awareness of what we are individually accepting as a truth. What we focus on creates our perspectives of reality; I experienced the first meditation with the gentleman because deep within my essence at that present time I wanted truth to show itself to me, thus allowing the spiritual being of the gentleman to manifest within my 'minds' eye.

What I saw in the meditation was my grandfathers' frequency/energy expressing itself to me, in a form that my mind could understand and accept at that given time, and my mind expressed it as he would have looked on the earth.

Consciousness expresses itself to us all in many forms, for example; light, sound, feeling, and anything visual. When working with spirit it is vitally important for your mind to be totally open, even when faced with new knowledge from your teachers, don't instantly rule it out as not to be true, try to be aware we are all independently resonating at our own different level of conscious awareness view and perspective, and that perspective is our point of understanding.

During your development what you experience, is from your point of awareness and understanding, and dependant of your attitude towards what the universe wants you to experience, you will not personally experience something if you are not willing to accept it as truth.

The one true thing that will honestly hold people back on their spiritual journey is ignorance of the human mind and ego; this is why it's very important to control your thoughts as regards to your spiritual path and life, because the same rules apply to both.

Eventually your spiritual life and private life will not be separate, because you will learn to understand what spirit teaches you, it will become your way of life. For many years up to the present day my spiritual path was not, and is not a religion to me. It is my way of life and through the teachings from spirit of unconditional love and Natural Law, I apply those teachings into my day to day life.

By Spencer
David
20-3-05

An early drawing Spencer David done of his grandfather in 2004

Chapter 3
Meeting my
Guide and
Family

On December 21st 2002 during the afternoon my mum received a phone call, and was given the very sad news that her sister Jean passed away. At times it doesn't matter how much you believe in spiritualism it does not make a loss of a loved one any easier to deal with.

A few hours later whilst we were at home, my mum, my Uncle Bill and I decided to have a sing on the Karaoke (badly I may add). When my mother walked back into the living room whilst I was singing she said," Oh can you smell that? It's Sherry." She suddenly said. "That's your auntie Jean that is, she always drank sherry." My mother called me over to see if I could smell it too. I took a big sniff thinking I wouldn't smell it, but it hit me very suddenly and I became very dizzy all of a sudden, which made me stumble backwards towards the arm chair behind me.

That was the first time I ever had smells like that from spirit, my Aunty Jean was trying to make it very clear that she had found her way around the spirit world, and obviously heard us on the karaoke and wanted to join in.

At this point within my development, now of around 2 years of sitting in a development circle, this was the first time my clairsentience acted quite strongly. When my aunt jean made contact with me I began to feel the sensation of drunkenness from the sherry, she connected with me with such conviction, my head began to spin more and I became unstable on my feet. I decided to hold on to the back of the arm chair nearby so I could steady myself, through the development I knew I had to tell her to take off the feeling from me, as it was too over powering, and very overwhelming. My aunt complied and removed the feelings from me, so I could get my bearings again.

When I came round a little more, I said to my mum "Jesus, how much of that stuff did she drink? 'Cus I feel as if I've had a full bottle!" shaking my head to try and clear it further, to my mums response "Well you know our Jean likes a party."

We began to talk about her then and bringing up old memories of what my mum and her brothers and sisters did when growing up, the little stories I have heard over the years, well those stories could be another book of their own.

42

Once Christmas was over and I was back at work, at the time I was working full time as a carer with clients that suffered from mental illnesses, such as Bi Polar Disorder and Schizophrenia with young adults. This helps various young adults live a fulfilling life with the support from a 24/7 care team, and is part of supported living, that was part of an integration into society program with the social services.

I can honestly say overall, it was a very rewarding job that has given me some very happy memories to cherish forever. Over time it did take a lot out of me, from long tiring hours because you have to constantly give your all, even on your bad days, so all you amazing carers in this world, I praise you all for your hard work in whatever area of care you are in. Keep it up because it is still Gods work you are doing, even if you haven't thought of it that way.

On a particular night shift when I was watching T.V. with my client, I went to sit down on the sofa and as I went to sit down I felt a single finger push me in the back, which made me slip off the chair. I knew what caused this, but obviously I could not tell my client, he looked at me very oddly so I had to make a fast joke about it, so I said "What am I like John" let's call him, "I slipped straight off that, it's all that Xmas booze getting to me" I commented jokingly, and we both laughed.

In my own mind, I had to say to spirit to stop it and be firm with them, or they will carry on with it.
During my evening shift with 'John' at work I kept picking up spontaneous smells of the drink sherry, at the similar time of getting the smells I noticed I was feeling quite drunk for a few seconds.

I knew precisely who it was trying to make a connection with me, my auntie Jean. I had to tell her to leave me alone and pester my mother, because it was costing me my concentration whilst I was helping 'John' to prepare dinner for us both.

For the next couple of weeks I noticed I was starting to get more of these smells and sensations of people standing behind me and I also started to see a lot more black shadows whizzing passed me which I could see out of the corner of my eye. These shadows were not the only thing I started to see, on occasions I saw orbs and spirit lights, they would float around in front of my face.

At first it did bug me and make me quit nervous, but eventually I started to get used to it, and it became quite comforting. I would talk either in my mind to them or out loud depending where I was. Orbs are a lovely thing to witness; they are spirit/loved ones energy, and what I was seeing is the etheric/spirit body expressing or showing itself as light energy, we all have this life force energy within us.

During this time while I was going to church in the open circle, I slowly started to get more and more information from spirit, for instance; pictures in my 'minds' eye, when I described to people what I was seeing; they started to relate to this information that I provided them with. I began to realised I was doing things and seeing things I could not explain and felt I needed some more insight to what I was doing.

During the time I spent sitting in development circles gathering further understanding on mediumship. I came to the realisation spiritual development was

something that is a continuous learning curve. During your own journey you will also notice this, and when you think it has fallen into place, further changes then come in to play, and you then will feel out of sorts again.
This is all quite normal, these challenging times in development keep you humble and is all part of your soul growth.

My mother and I made a booking with a medium called Stephanie Jenkins as I told my mum she was very good. Stephanie mentioned various things my mother was going through at the time; Stephanie made contact with a couple of members of our family for my mum including her mum and dad. During the reading Stephanie made a contact with a little girl in spirit, of whom my mum miscarried many years previous, who had never come through before in a reading. My mum was very pleased with her reading, and I can still remember her smiling to herself as she came out of the room.

We began to chat for a couple of moments, and then it was my turn for a reading. As I walked into the room there was soft gentle music playing very quietly in the background; that set a very peaceful and calming environment.

I sat down and Stephanie began the reading, my grandparents, on my mother's side made a brief appearance and gave me some clarification about various elements within my own early development, with some praise of my efforts.

Stephanie continued with the reading and became aware of a gentleman, as she described at first, as a young foreign man who is going to help me on my spiritual path, and he was here to introduce himself to me. "This man is really tall, around 6 feet 7 inches with a strong build" Stephanie proclaimed. "He is of a Native American origin, and he has a head band with a single feather, pocking out to the right of his head" she continued.

Stephanie then suggested we do a brief meditation, instructed by my guide so I could see and greet him, I remember the sheer excitement of meeting one of my guides, I knew I had them, but at this point in my development, he had never shown himself, or identified himself to me. I was asked to close my eyes and relax, which I was very much used to doing.

I remember Stephanie telling me to visualise myself by a river, an image in my mind began to take form after around a minute or two. I could see I was on a river bank in a location I was unfamiliar with. Stephanie told me I will see a canoe in the river, and to get into it, so I did.

I began to gently float down the river; very calmly the water was softly encouraging me forwards, the sky was so blue with some light clouds, randomly scattered around within the view of my mind. The sun was also shining gently upon me; I could even feel a gentle breeze on my face, as I became completely overtaken by the experience and went with it, without any doubt within my mind because I knew I was going to meet my guide.

I proceeded down the river taking in the scenery of mountains views, the canoe began to slow down and come to a stop as it approached a cove. As I stopped at the bank I could see a figure of a male waiting for me. At first I could only see a shadow of a very tall and broad male because the sun was shining over his shoulder.

As I approached this gentleman I began to feel an energy that I felt was familiar and I had felt, and made contact with it before. I got closer, and details began to emerge, this man had a band in his hair, just like Stephanie said. He had long hair; muscular build, dark skinned and I could see he was a Native American, standing very proud, with a firm, stern look upon his face.

Not the most approachable looking person I had met, but I had a calming, protective feeling come over me. "Hum." He says, and then gives me his name "I am Running Deer". We went on a short walk and discussed a few things; unfortunately though it was time to come back before I knew it.

Stephanie guided me back out of the meditation and asked how I was. "Wonderful" I said, "I met my Native guide Running Deer, it's him, he has been with me, for the past two years." I explained.

We eventually joined my mum and we had another talk before my mother and I left. My mum didn't give Stephanie a name about the child, but as we left the house and headed home in her car, the name Rosie came to my mother's mind.

When my mother and I got home, my mum phoned Stephanie back to tell her what had happened, and Stephanie explained that it was spirit that placed the name into her mind to let her know what she wants to be called.

I continued going to the open circle and things started to go really well for me concerning my spiritual development. I went to the church on the Monday to sit in circle, while I was meditating a little girl came to me and she was around 5 or 6 years old. She stood in front of me with her head down and her eyes looking up at me. I could see her eyes were ocean blue and she was wearing a purple velvet dress with a white collar.

The little girl I could see had lovely brown hair in two pigtails at either side of her head, with three freckles on each cheek, that if you connected them it would create an upside down triangle.

Suddenly during my meditation I heard "Hello, I'm Rosie." Well this came to me as a bit of a shock and I got quite emotional, a little tear came to my eye and I could feel a lump in my throat form. I couldn't believe it, it was Rosie, the little girl my mum lost and also came through in the reading to my mum a couple of days previous.

It was a brief encounter with her, but still a very pleasant surprise. Rosie started to tell me she was with my grandmother and she was fine and to pass her love on to my mum. At the end of the open circle the church had a little raffle every week.

The leader of the group asked me to draw out a ticket, so I pulled one out, and it was number 216. I called out the number to see who had won and no one answered. A lady sitting next to me then asked me to check my ticket, so I went into my pocket and checked the numbers I had, I unfolded it and what a shock… it was my own ticket I called out.

I went to collect my prize, and there were a few things there like chocolates, air freshener and there was a little square box which contained a broach with a flower on it. As I looked at the broach I thought my mum would like that, so that was what I chose.

I got home and I told my mum about what happened at the church, and explained the meditation, and Rosie made an appearance. My mum was very pleased that Rosie came through to me, to pass on her love, and then I told her about the raffle, and told her I had won.

I passed her the box and she opened it, she said, "Ah that's lovely bab, thank you." Then suddenly she said, "Hang-on, have you looked at this properly?"
"No, why?" I replied.
"Well there is a rose on this broach." So I took a look at it and without a doubt, there was the rose. Instantly I knew spirit was confirming to us they were pleased with the name, and that we should keep calling her by this.

I continued with the open circle and things were going well, after a few weeks it became apparent that Rosie was making regular contact during meditations and also whilst I was at home. At the beginning it started off with her just coming to me at the church and giving me messages.

Over time Rosie started coming to me in the meditations, to tell me that I will win the raffle. I would buy the ticket, take a seat and once I sat down she would then say if I will win the raffle or not.
I never asked her to tell me if I was going to win the raffles, it was Rosie's way of building a contact and trust through the gentle teasing with the raffle like a child playing a game with her. Even though Rosie is

giving me small pieces of information like this, doesn't mean they will tell me I will win the lottery.

After a few more weeks Rosie started to visit me at home and she would sit on my lap when I was watching T.V. When Rosie sat with me; I would feel very cold from her energy presence, with a light pressure as if a small child was sitting on your lap now, but with much less pressure and weight.

Rosie also showed me her energy around my house, by allowing me to see orbs. Orbs are a projection of light, from their light body, and seeing these light anomalies is possible through clairvoyance. This became very regular for about 3 months, then she began coming to me at times when I went to a healing at the church, and brought my dogs with her from spirit. I would be sitting there all relaxed and then I would see her in my 'minds' eye.

The level of contact with Rosie has become less and less of late, but she has managed on two or three occasions to speak through me in trance, from around the time of 2015 to this present day.

Chapter 4
Visit from a Light Being

At this point I am now around three years into my development, and receiving contact from spirit more regularly. At this stage I was managing to string messages together with some evidence of the communicator, and the reason they make contact, meaning passing on a message to the receiver.

This next random occasion with spirit happened one morning at a friends' house, I had slept over, the night previous. I was sleeping on the sofa, and suddenly I heard three knocks on the glass of the French double doors he had.

The moment I heard the knock I turned my head to the right to look at the door, to see who it was, and in the window of the door there was a quite solid looking figure glowing in gold, standing and waving at me with both hands.

This figure as what I can only describe as a golden glowing light figure, very similar to the light being in the 80's movie Cocoon. I began to stare at it whilst the being of light continued to wave at me with a high level of excitement and joy, possibly because I can see them.

At first I slowly sat up on the sofa without blinking, and turned my body to face the figure. My eyes were locked on, as I didn't want to miss anything, I was so stunned and amazed I could see something so beautiful shimmering in gold.

The being had a lighter gold auric field; it was like a golden haze, just like you see on a hot day, the haze hovering from the surface off the road. The gold translucent aura was shimmering approximately 2 to 3 inches around the whole of its body. What I was looking at was light energy; it was very solid like, and it wasn't as transparent as other contacts from spirit I had seen before.

The figure was standing around 5ft 10 inches tall, but hovering above 8 to 10 inches from the floor. I could see their feet glowing but they were not on the ground. I began to get up very calmly and make my way closer to the door, and then I began to see features on its face. Very basic looking features, enough to know it had a mouth, normal size nose, eyes, and these details were in slightly darker shades of gold to the rest of its body, to create the shape and contours of the face.

I continued to walk forward so I could open the door, again I felt very calm with this energy, but as I went to open the door it smiled with a very cheeky feel to it, which made me giggle and laugh with it.

I grabbed the door handle to open the door and suddenly the light being began to float out of my view to my right. I opened the door to follow it and I suddenly noticed, it was moving in a running motion. The legs and arms of the light being where moving as you would whilst running, but floating and heading towards the corner of the house and went out of sight. I very quickly followed after it to see where it was heading, as I got to the corner of the house to turn to my right and look, it vanished within a moment.

I was alone the whole time, I went back into the house to try and figure out what precisely just happened, what I would say lasted no longer than a minute. I returned to the sofa and sat down, for a few moments I was confused but I knew I had to ask the universe what just happened.

Within an instant a gentle whisper entered my mind "That was spirit." Of course like many of you will appreciate if you are on a spiritual journey, we question the spirit world and the universe many times on many occasions such as "was that real?" Or "was that my imagination?"

Questioning everything is precisely what we must always do, without questions, we get no answers and therefore we shall not grow and expand in understanding, neither shall we understand lies from truth.

For a couple of moments I had doubts of what I heard, as I could not at that moment get my head around what I had just witnessed. Once again I questioned my spirit team "Ok spirit, if that experience was from you, I need more proof."

Acting in this manner is not being disrespectful towards spirit or the universe when they interact with us. Our purpose is to seek truth, and asking the spirit world/universe to provide proof of that, so you can see the truth for yourself is absolutely fine.

Once I had asked for proof from spirit, their reply was "Go to circle today, and you will receive your answer." I fully accepted their offer, so I gathered my things and headed home to get ready for the open circle, which was later on in the afternoon.

I got to the church around 1.15pm, so I had time to compose myself, looking back at times people may have thought I was being rude or ignorant, but after sitting with spirit for the couple of years, I had bought myself to a point where I was taking my development very seriously.

From a very early phase in my development I knew what I was learning was something not to be taken lightly. When you are developing you will come to an understanding that what we do, is not just for ourselves, and most definitely not for entertainment or fame, but it is for our own personal growth and for the growth of humanity. In time all the spiritual teachings and principles you have been taught by spirit become your way of life not your religion.

Your spiritual growth takes dedication and personal responsibility from yourself to help others, there is a huge emotional responsibility in mediumship, and the role of a medium is something that should be taken very seriously and handled with complete respect at all times. It is your moral obligation to do so whilst working with spirit.

When connecting to the spirit world to pass on messages, you are not connecting with just a person on the earth, and a loved one in spirit; you are connecting to their souls. You are connecting to someone upon the earth that maybe dealing with grief on the deepest level you can't imagine. Grief is something that affects us all differently, and depending on who has passed over, depends on how deep that wound of the heart is.

As a medium people come to you for strength, upliftment, direction and most of all peace of mind, we have to have compassion and understanding whilst delivering a message. You are dealing with people's emotions; my rule in mediumship to me is to pass on a message the way you would like to receive one. Mediumship should come from a place of unconditional love. Pure genuine mediumship comes from our soul, and through our heart centre, and never from the human ego.

I had got myself settled, water, raffle etc. the circle was opened with a prayer and we sang a hymn. Then we were asked to settle our minds and go into a short unguided meditation listening to peaceful music, gently in the background.

On this occasion I never received a message to pass on; I was meditating within the energy of my guide

Running Deer, we were not communicating as such, but just sitting to increase our blending, to further my mediumship, and to help discipline my mind. Disciplining the mind is paramount, as time goes on this aids you to work in deeper states of consciousness, this will be for the purpose of Trance mediumship, or sitting for Physical Mediumship.

The meditation lasted around 15 to 20 minutes, we were lightly guided back to our own awareness, and people were asked to share what they had, in a round robin style format. 3 or 4 people passed on messages, but nothing for me as of yet, about confirming anything as to what I experienced that morning.

Finally I got my answer, from the last person in the circle, talk about keeping me waiting, I thought. A young lad in his early 20s stood up, I knew this young man now for a little while, and he had been sitting in the same circle as me for around the same length of time. He announced "Spencer, may I come to you please?" "Of course" I responded politely.

He gave me some evidence of the communicator he had with him, it was my mums' dad. He went on to say "Spencer he is telling me you had a new experience this morning." I instantly burst out a short laugh and replied "You could say that." still chuckling to myself.

He followed on to say "Well why are you doubting? You know its Spirit, and now they are confirming it to you." then said "And that is all they are asking me to pass on, God bless." The message was finished there, and of course people became intrigued.

When I first went into the church, I didn't tell anybody anything of that morning, so I could confirm it was spirit. It is very easy to share your life to people in the churches you greet, but when going to circle, we really should try not to give too much of ourselves away.

This is so when we do get a message you can tell it's from spirit, and not cause Chinese whispers, or something that can potentially be created in the mediums mind, for over hearing what people are talking about.

This is why when mediums do church services; they should not be sitting in the church and mingling with people, prior to their service of clairvoyance. Mediums are deliberately sat in a separate room so they cannot pick up conversations from the congregation as the medium can be accused of acting fraudulently as they can potentially listen into conversations and use that information during the service. Whilst sitting in a private room it also gives the medium a chance to prepare themselves, for the clairvoyance and philosophy they will do in the service.

After many years of self-development and research I am now at the right level of understanding to explain what happened on the day I have previously just described.
The whole main reason for writing this book is to make the reader aware that everything comes from consciousness and energy, and everything is an expression of consciousness, hence the title choice for this book.

I now have had the time to reflect upon many occasions I have spent connecting with the Spirit World, and due to the time spent sitting and listening to my guides/spirit team and gathering further experiences with them, I can now explain to you as the reader my understanding of what happened.

This was something that was not possible 15 years ago, due to my own lack of understanding of the workings behind spirit communication, understanding of the Spirit World and us.

What I experienced was not clairvoyance because the 'Being' physically appeared outside the house in the back garden as an objective physical manifestation/ materialisation of its light body, and would have been visible to anybody that was present. If I had seen the contact clairvoyantly, it would have only been me that would have seen it or those that are clairvoyant, because the etherical being would be allowing them to seen in that manner through clairvoyance.

However, this then would not be a full materialisation meaning. If I was with my friend who I was staying with and they had also seen the manifestation, and witnessed its physical appearance that it showed me, regardless of them being clairvoyant or not, that's a materialisation, or physical manifestation of spirit, and not the use of clairvoyance. The light 'Being' had slowed their vibrational frequency down, making them appear more solid, therefore becoming visible to the human eye.

From sitting with my guides they have bought my awareness to now understanding, that this was a full materialisation of the light body of that particular Being. As previously mentioned that everything is energy, energy can show and express itself to us how ever it chooses to look, and the mind interprets its appearance accordingly.

Those interpretations and ideologies can be bought on by many influences placed upon us whilst we live in this 3D world in a 4D reality. 3D = Physical Body/World and 4D = Time. So 3D (Physical) + 4D (time) making us live in a 4D reality. (4th Dimension).

You need to understand that you are a Multi-dimensional, Multi-conscious, Multi-verse of a Spiritual Being, vibrating in a human body, living in a human existence, and this all happens because everything is powered by Consciousness.

We can live without our physical body, but we cannot exist without Consciousness; the intelligent life source of energy that created everything.

What had to happen for the materialisation to take place? For a full materialisation or manifestation of a spirit light body, they have to do a number of things to allow this to happen. One of the main things they have to do so we can see them is to slow down their vibrational frequency, slowing it down allows them to change form.

Slowing down their vibration enough, allows them to appear as physical matter, this creates changes to their form, and manifest a physical body, or to appear as whatever ever the spirit world is materialising.
By the light being slowing his/her frequency down, thus slowing down its vibration, allows the etherical body to express its form of appearance into our 3D/4D world/reality. Once the spirit contact has lowered or slowed down their vibration enough, this is when they

become visible to the naked human eye, and everybody in that area will see whatever has taken form.

Those in the Spirit World vibrate at a much higher and faster vibration of frequency than what we do, whilst we are within our physical body. This is why spirit does not have a physical body, because they are vibrating or living in an etherical world, which exists amongst and around us all.

Due to the difference in vibration of their living reality and ours, their world cannot interfere with ours, but what we believe, and what ideologies we have or believe to be true, can create that temporary environment when we return to spirit.

The reason for certain planes that we live within the Spirit World, are temporary to us, this is because when we gather more understanding through the observation of truth, we move further forward on our journeys spiritual growth. The Ideologies and belief structures that hold back our growth of consciousness and soul, that we pick up in our physical path, such as beliefs like religion, is moved away from us. This is because these ideologies and beliefs no longer serve our souls purpose. Also it is a man-made construct for mass control and divide. Religion does not apply within the World of Spirit, and also religion does not follow Natural law.

For instance a person that believes in a particular religion will have experiences related to that religious belief structure but over time from the world of spirit, these beliefs will move away from that person, once they have chosen to leave this limitation of growth.

The Spirit World where our loved ones return back to is a world that has no limitations. It's a world working on the basis of light, thought, frequency, vibration and unconditional love. Once returned to spirit, they have to follow natural law; this state of awareness allows them to seek further purpose and truth. All of this exists alongside us within the same existence of consciousness.

The Universe and the spirit world is a vast environment that has many planes of understanding and Dimensions, when we pass over to the spirit world we change back to our natural form, which is the light body or etheric body.

On this principle it is the reason why when we as mediums connect to spirit, we have to raise our frequency through setting our own intention to do so; this will happen naturally once you set to raise your own consciousness through meditation.

Using techniques to open chakras is not needed, this is misinformation, and you cannot open or close chakras. Chakras are energy receptors within our etherical body that are constantly vibrating and sending energy throughout our being.
Each chakra serves a purpose to help the smooth running of our physical bodies. For 15 years I was told to open chakras so I could contact spirit, but when I started to do guided meditations in trance with my guides, they were not opening or closing chakras during meditation, and through this I have found the opening and closing of chakras not possible.

This is because energy must always flow, if energy stops moving this is when problems can occur within our physical body and can cause dis-ease. Hence you cannot close chakras; our energy is connected to the Universal Consciousness permanently through the workings of our central nervous system, cutting off from that life force energy would be a major problem. Cutting off from the Universal Consciousness would be like you trying to run your personal computer once taking out its processor unit first from the motherboard.

This brief description below is a break down about the seven Planes in the Spirit World, this was something I came across early in my development and resonates with me at my current level of understanding of truth as I have personally visited and experienced one of these levels through meditation and meeting a friend. The description below has been recently provided to me by a friend who is a trance medium called Aiden Hall. This information was given to him via his own guide Jacob, of whom both have given me the permission to publish this information; this is why I have credited them both into my book.

The First Plane - The Earth Plane is far denser than the astral planes, and contains Lower Vibrations. Those that are attached to certain people stay on this plane, and those who can't accept that they have died stay attached to where it is familiar, from life in the physical.

The Second Plane - The Astral Plane. The Astral Plane has two main levels, firstly the lower astral plane is dark and eerie Buddhists would call it 'Bardo' and Catholics would call it 'Purgatory'. Edgar Cayce called it 'The Plane of Darkness'. Whilst on this plane those here go through a period of intense reflection, this helps further understanding to each soul that has left the Earth Plane.

Secondly the upper level of the Astral Plane is lighter, less dense because the vibration is much faster and is more of a halfway station between Earth and the spirit world. It's a travelling plane.

The Third plane - Plane of Illusion – This Plane is very similar to Earth, it is a beautiful and peaceful and a very Earth-like setting. People live in houses and 'work'. They also eat and drink, and carry on in an idealised version of Earth with but with no sickness.

Every pleasure the heart desires is crested by the mind and satisfied. Want cake? Poof ... your mind makes a cake appear, that kind of thing. The majority of souls here have manifested their environment on this level to mirror their religious beliefs on Earth. It's sort of a self-fulfilling prophecy.

For example a Catholic would expect to see golden gates and St. Peter open them, then this manifests at this level which has all come from the mind created by the ideologies and belief structures taught on Earth. For other examples; if a Muslim man expects to be greeted by a group of virgin women serving him grapes on a golden platter, this then manifests at this level. A Baptist might expect to have a city filled with only Baptists so that's what he finds there. This may sound great but it really is stagnant and will not allow the soul to ascend in further understanding. The soul has a choice and must either return to earth to learn and grow, or it has to learn to move on to the fourth plane and grow from there.

The Fourth Plane - World of Idealised Form - All desires for Earthly contact disappear, the soul explores beyond the confines of the earthly plane, thus expanding thoughts and knowledge of which are not held down by wants of sex, chocolate, cake or "Baptist only' cloud cities or any other desire that was considered 'heavenly' in the third plane.

Reincarnation is no longer necessary; the soul is free of dogmas and rigid intellectual structures. This creates freedom to access energies not available in the planes lower than this; this is the plane that the soul is finding   true   freedom   on.

Fifth Plane - Plane of Flame - The soul takes on the body of a flame. (Or a form; like a flame). It can travel the universe (universes) without any physical or spiritual harm. It can grow in understanding and while it still retains its individuality, it becomes part of a 'group soul'. A group soul for example; Spirits who vibrate at the same level and/or who are at the same level of understanding through what the soul has learnt over time, and a vast understanding of the universe etc. will naturally become drawn together.

Sixth Plane - Plane of Light - Evolved souls. Souls that have ascended here have lived through all aspects of the created universe and have completed their growth process. They have no need for matter or form and exist purely as 'white light' and emotion is absent. They are so in line with the creator that they become the pure thought of the creator. This actually matches up to what some of the Catholic saints have said about souls in heaven becoming so instep with God that they almost disappear and that they are joined to God. The Catholic Church doesn't talk about all these planes, but some of what is being said is similar to St. John of the Cross and St. Teresa of Avila, along with many others from over the years.

Seventh Plane - Plane of the Spirit Realm - The

domain of God (or the Creator). The soul here loses form and becomes One with God.

Chapter 5
Visiting the Spirit World

The ending of last chapter leads me to write about two wonderful experiences with spirit that validates the previous information regarding the description of the seven Planes of the Spirit World. The two experiences are over two separate time periods the first experience was very much out of the blue and unexpected and the second was through a meditation.

On the first occasion, it was an early evening and my mother and I had not long eaten, we were watching one of our usual classic comedy programmes together and the phone rang. My mum answered and began a conversation. I continued to carry on watching because I knew my mum would now be on the phone a while, as she loved her chats with friends and family, and keeping up-to-date with everything.

At this point I was not paying too much attention of what my mum was saying, as I was too busy chuckling to myself with whatever I was watching at the time on TV. Suddenly though my ears pricked up when my mum said "How strange I wonder what that was?" for this part of the book I will keep the person on the phone anonymous so I will call the person 'Jenny' or 'Jen' there will also be references to a 'Jacob' and an 'Emily', these names are of children that I have also changed the names of.

My mum continued to say "But the candle flames should all go in the same direction, was there a window open?" I turned to my mother and said "What you on about?" My mum then explained to me that 'Jenny' had got a birthday cake for one of her children and the candle flames were "Acting weird" when the cake was placed on the table.

I did ask if there was a door or window open that could have caused a cross wind and changed the direction of one or two candle flames. My mums reply was "One half of the candle flames went one way to the left, and the other half went the other to the right." "And no one was blowing on them?" I asked.

At this point the phone was put on loud speaker so I could now hear Jenny talking, and then I heard Jenny say "I just put it on the table as we were singing happy birthday to Jacob, and he was just sitting there waiting, plus there is no way he can blow them in two different directions he is 8, not Superman." Of which my mother and I started laughing quite loudly.

After the hard belly bursting laugh from Jennys' Superman comment the three of us just had, I then suggested it could be spirit. "But who would that be?" My mother replied. I responded with "It could be Anny or whatever that girls name is that you know that just passed, Jacobs' friend?"

"Oh you mean Emily." Jenny said "Yes that's right." I confirmed. From there my mum started talking about that possibility, as I went quiet because I very quickly became aware of a cold feeling gently coming in towards me from my left hand side which triggered a reaction from our dog. At the time we would have had our pet dog around 5 months from 10/12 weeks old. She was a Rottweiler and was as soft as putty and as daft as a brush, but when my guides or spirit showed up, she would always sit upright and give two big barks and lay back down. You would then see her eyes following them around the house, but eventually she got used to it.

The energy that came close instantly felt like the presence of a child, I began to concentrate as my mum and Jenny continued talking over the loud speaker. I made them aware that I had someone with me, but at that moment not knowing who. It wasn't long before I put two and two together and figured out who it was, as I had previously met this child on several occasions.

'Emily' was friend a of 'Jacob' as his parents were very close friends with the young girls parents, so they all spent quite some time together. Emily had sadly passed a couple of months previous after suddenly collapsing in her school playground due to a heart condition. I am aware this child and family were very aware and clear about her condition and strict measures where followed as much as possible, and 'play' unfortunately came with risks.

Emily couldn't play like other children; she couldn't freely run around and play sport, or even ride a bike, so imagine at times it must have been highly frustrating for her watching her friends play and knowing her potential fate. I am unfamiliar with all the finer details of the incident but I do know through conversations Emily 'chose' to join in a game of 'tag', which very sadly was the last thing she got to do.

This little girl was around seven years old and I could start seeing her taking form in my mind clairvoyantly, at first I couldn't see all her features as there was a very strong bright light of gold behind her, as she began to show herself to me. As the gold translucent light glowing behind her began to dim slightly, it created her features to become clearer and more apparent.

I could see her hair and her facial features as I noticed her standing with a smile on her face, with a feel of extreme excitement as it was her contact with 'Jenny'. I started to inform jenny and my mum of what I was receiving, to what I hear Jenny say "What Emily is there with you?" "Yes" I replied. "Very much so." I confirmed.

As her image progressively manifested clearer within my mind Emily confirmed "It was me that moved the flames on Jacobs' cake." She announced "It's also me that sets off Buzz Light-year at the top of the stairs." The little innocent voice in my mind explained. "To infinity and beyond!" She suddenly shouted.

I then suddenly heard Jenny shout over the loud speaker on the phone "Oh my God!" "That's what the bloody toy says." Jenny said sharply with a shocked tone in her voice. "Tell her to stop doin' it, it freaks me out" she explained. Emily apologised for frightening her and it was not her intention to do so.

As I continued to pass on other pieces of personal information to Jenny, Emily confirmed she was at peace where she was and also informed Jenny of her visiting other members of the family on Earth from the world of spirit. Emily told us that she had been trying to make her presence felt at her parents' home over the previous months. Unfortunately Emily was having difficulty due to her parents' beliefs and not paying attention to the signs Emily was providing.

Jenny asked the little girl what it was like where she was in the spirit world, to Emilys' reply "Where I am is a place of pure beauty, a place of peace and Unconditional love." Emily used my tools of clairvoyance and clairaudience to explain to my mother and Jenny what it was like.

Emily said to me within my mind gently, like a whisper fluttering into the forefront of my consciousness "I am now going to show you what my world is like, and I want you to tell them everything you can see." I replied back to her in my mind through thought "Ok of course." To speak to our loved ones in spirit we don't necessarily have to speak out loud. The spirit world is an etherical world and their communication is through thought and vibrational energy, through the workings of the infinite network field of consciousness.

I explained to my mum and Jenny what was about to happen, so they sat quiet with the phone still on loud speaker as I began to explain in detail of what I was seeing and experiencing. As I stood up in front of my mum in the middle of the living room to stand closer to the phone. I was gently closing my eyes as I heard my dog get up and walk towards me, I looked towards her and gave her a smile as she approached me and then I gently rubbed her head.

I stood upright to start concentrating on what was about to take place, I then became aware my dog decided to lay on the floor leaning against my right leg and settled within the energy that was becoming stronger around me. Emily was still standing to my left side as her gentle loving energy overlapped the dog, I remembered dogs are far more aware of energy and can see spirit far greater than the majority of us are able to, in fact all animals can, their minds are not clouded with the high level of ignorance the human mind has. Animals are on a different level of consciousness to humans and they are naturally clairvoyant and attuned to picking up and receiving energy, as they are far more closely linked to Mother Nature than we generally are.

I closed my eyes as the room became silent I quickly coughed just to clear my throat as the energy of Emily starts shifting around me. Within my own mind I begin to feel the energy in my head and around me expanding outwards as my vibration within me quickens I am raising my conscious point of awareness to connect with that of Emilys' point of awareness.

In order for Emily to allow me to experience her world I have to blend my consciousness with it, when this happens this alters my state of awareness and takes me a little deeper, but this is not trance as I was aware of what I was explaining. What is happening is I have been put into more of a 'meditative state' which heightens my senses, and enables me to get the feelings and sensations, far stronger than I would in an ordinary one to one sitting.

As I continue to focus, I start to feel lighter, less dense almost as if I was standing in front of my mum in my own astral/ light body and I didn't feel my physical form. In my mind Emily began describing her world and experiences, and showing me various things at the same time.
As mentioned in the previous chapter, what I am seeing is Emilys' personal experience of the spirit world. What I was shown is from her conscious point of awareness and is an expression of what her mind has created within that plane of the spirit world. These experiences are based on her beliefs and ideologies given to her through her upbringing and her individual perspective of truth, all of us who pass over have their own individual experience of the spirit world also.

She took me back to the day she passed, not to the scene more to do with her phases of entering the world of spirit. She suddenly says to me "I saw those big gold gates the man told me about at church, they're massive." She said with great enthusiasm, as I heard it, I gently smiled as a bolt of emotion came rushing up through from my heart into my throat.

I had to take a gasp of air as the feeling completely overwhelmed me, I suddenly said to my mum "Oh my God she is going to make me cry." as my throat gets a lump within it making it difficult for me to speak. I pulled my glasses away from my face as my eyes welled up; with my eyes still closed I wiped them with my sleeve of my jumper, to remove the tears that had started to fall down both cheeks of my face.

At that moment in my mind I rapidly started to see the most beautiful a clearest of blue skies I have ever seen in my entire life. Then two clouds one from my left view in my mind, and one from the right pull slowly together. As the clouds begin to move to the centre of the view in my 'minds' eye, a sun begins to gently form in the centre of the two clouds, with the tips of each cloud not touching, as the sun poked through them uninterrupted.

As I looked down I was suddenly standing on a cobbled path I looked forward and like Emily said about the gates I could see them in the distance, they looked like they went up into the sky and disappeared within the clouds. The top of the gates were out of view due to the brightness of the sun shining downwards towards the path, lightening it up in all its glory before me.

I began to explain to my mum and Jenny what I was seeing I gently heard from the phone "Wow how beautiful." Emily begins explaining to me. "That's what I saw when I left the play-ground and an angel came for me, and showed me the way, he was kind and gentle, I felt very safe with him."

Within my consciousness Emily proceeded to show me what she saw and experienced behind the gates, I moved forwards through the gates quite quickly and I was standing in a huge meadow, I could see for miles endless beautiful scenes of nature and many different animals.

"I love butterflies, rainbows and unicorns, that is why I see them, don't you know?" Emily says to me with confidence and sheer joy in her words as I hear them within in mind. "It's beautiful; it's amazing…..it's…. it's unbelievable." I reply to her out loud. I relay back to Jenny and my mum what I was hearing and seeing, and trying to keep them informed as much as possible, at the same time as I am trying to take it all in without breaking down in tears because it was so overwhelming with emotion, and total unconditional love.

I began to take in the view within my mind and have a look around of the breath taking scenery, I could see for miles around me. We were standing in the middle of the most beautiful meadow I'd even seen; the colours were so more vibrant than our world, so much more colour, each colour stood out more than the last. The sky was like a pearl blue as I looked at the clouds they looked much sharper, I could see every layer of the cloud formed so perfectly and of the purest white they almost had a 'glow' to them as they hovered above in various shapes and sizes.

The blades of grass were gently swaying left and right, the softest of breezes glides past us, I feel it gently stroke past my face with such grace and elegance. Each blade of grass is shimmering and sparkling in a magnificent colour of Emerald green. The grass was so bright and shiny it was like we were walking on an untouched lawn made from a soft bed of emerald crystals, I could see many beings walking around happy and relaxed; some were skipping and acting joyful with each other and some just quietly gathered sharing thoughts expanding their awareness.

The scene kept changing, as soon as I got used to one environment it changed to another, Emily began to explain, that where ever she wants to go it can be created within her mind and she is placed there. She then explained, through me to Jenny and my mum, because she liked the band 'Take That' she can project her energy through the infinite 'time loops' in the Quantum Universe and place herself back to a previous concert and 'relive' it all over again.

When Emily takes herself to that time frame, and experience, she can experience all the joys of the atmosphere, very much like it is on Earth. Emily told me she had been to a concert before she passed away prior her heart diagnosis, and her experience in the world of spirit at the concert felt 'just as real'.

"I had to go hospital when I first arrived in Spirit." Emily suddenly addressed. "What was that like?" I asked her. "A lot cleaner and less waiting time." she said with a snigger and began to explain to us some of the process. It's very different they didn't put me in an ambulance like on earth, Emily was met by one or two members of her family and she saw a bright white light and got in an 'Egg shaped light pod' and was met by The Healers of Light. They are your equivalent of doctors but they administer us with frequency healing not medication she explained.

Emily continued to explain whilst in the light pod they gave her some healing and this frequency of energy is for them to become relaxed and settled whilst they have other things explained to them. I was told this 'Light Pod' was big and had other people that had also passed and each of them had a healing team of 3 members. The first is an 'Overseer' and was wearing golden colour clothes. The second member is a counsellor wearing white, and the third administered the frequency was wearing green. I was informed Emily seen 'machines' she was unfamiliar with and looked very different to equipment our hospitals use, these showed lots of information and were far 'more advanced'.

Emily explained she was sitting on very 'posh recliner' type chair that could move and be completely flat if needed, she described that her chair wasn't laid out flat as she was comfortable enough with the position it was in. The healer administered the frequency healing by placing their hand on the back of her left hand, and the energy was applied.
Emily described when the healing was in process there was a 'bright glow' of blue light coming out of the side of his hand which made her hand glow blue and started to feel the energy pass through his hand and up her arm, and then throughout her spirit body.

I was told the blue represented peace and tranquillity to her because that was one of her favourite colours, the healer 'knew' all about Emily from the moment of her arrival. Due to Emily loving the colour blue that was why that colour was used, and will be different for everybody on their transition to the Spirit World.

Emily concluded that when she arrived at the hospital in Spirit, further healing was done in order for her to accept and understand various elements of what the soul needed work on, in forms of lessons, removing blockages and conditions, creating clarity and bringing further understanding of truth. Emily confirmed this has to be done in order for the soul to grow into a new point of awareness.
I began to feel myself getting tired and the energy was starting to fade, I told my mum and Jenny, Emily was

bringing the link to an end and I proceeded to come back to my own awareness as all the things in my 'minds' eye began to disappear. Emily closed the communication and passed on her love, and then the coldness on my left dispersed I opened my eyes looked around the room with my dog still lying by my side gently resting against my leg.

As I moved to sit down a take a drink the dog moved and looked at me as if to say 'Thanks for waking me up.' I spoke to Jenny to get feedback and she was still a little dumb struck, to be honest so was I, and also now feeling quite tired, so I left them to finish off the phone call, and I went to my room to relax and recharge.

At that point what had happened was a mind blowing experience and I thought I can't wait for that to happen again. The next time I visited the Spirit world was through a meditation where I met a friend called Richard that had passed over a couple of years previously.

Richard was a local man I knew growing up in my area, he lived alone and was an alcoholic and there were times I visited Richard to have a couple of drinks with him and watch the football, snooker or just to talk about many things to keep him company. At the time I was going there, I was still dealing with my own grief from Paul passing over.

Although Richard had drink issues, he was a very intelligent man, whom many people didn't see, apart from his friends he knew from his local. There was around a 30 year age gap between us, but then I have always been drawn to mix with older people. One of his small joys was to buy various newspapers for the cryptic crosswords and puzzle games of which he always finished with ease, and 'catch up with the worlds lies" I used to laugh when he said that, as I was never one for reading the newspapers.

Richard and I had a good friendship, he knew my mum and thought very highly of her, and he always showed the upmost respect to her, and women in general. He was a wise soul and always gave sound advice even though he may not have handled his own affairs correctly, but who am I to judge, I still had a lot of respect for him regardless, and a lot to learn myself.

Before Richard died I managed to have a couple of conversations with him, and used to talk to him a lot about Paul, and tell him what Paul and I had been up to. Like the time I went to the gym with him and Paul nearly killed me by overloading the bench press which I couldn't lift, and making me do 5 sets of 10 reps, doing dumbbell curls. Richards response to this memory was "There is nothing on you, you couldn't bench press a bag of sugar." then we had a good laugh about it.

I also asked Richard what his thoughts were on the afterlife, and he told me on many occasions over the years, that he heard his own mother call him in the mornings, after she passed. He wasn't sure what to believe but because he had some experiences with his own mother, he told me. "There must be something out there, and if there is when I die I'll come back and tell you." He brushed that comment off with a laugh and we both had a chuckle about what he might be like in the Spirit World, and he joked "Yeah I am just gonna haunt the horrible bastards left behind." He was blunt sometimes like that but I got it, that was just his dark humour and mine was no better at the time.

Our humour was very suited and I have many great memories from laughing with him, we had many interesting conversations about all sorts to do with life, we even discussed the possibility of aliens no doubt. My experience was very different with Richard than it was with Emily it happened during one of my regular meditation sittings, when I used to meditate around 4pm every afternoon.

I began, like any other meditation, relaxing myself and clearing my mind, I would just sit in my own energy with music playing in the background. Once I feel relaxed enough I start raising my thoughts towards the spirit world, and connect with the guide who chooses to come forward. On this particular occasion I became aware of my Native guide making a connection to me, as I feel his energy come close and cocoon me gently.

All of a sudden I felt my energy within me begin to 'quicken' this is the feeling you can get when you raise your consciousness and your vibration speeds up, when connecting with spirit, or your own guides.

I noticed myself feeling much lighter as I began raising my conscious awareness; at this point I was aware I was 'out of my body' and in the etherical realms with Running Deer as we began to astral travel within this infinite world of consciousness. A place where we are limitless and free to travel where ever the soul wants to take us.

The Etherical World/Spirit World is a place based on thoughts, our reality and environment can change with a blink of the eye, from a simple, single thought. As I was flying through, a blue, beautiful sky above the clouds, which felt like I was there for ages, I could see I was flying above houses and I could see the patchwork effect of the fields below, as I soared above freely without worry or fear. I became engulfed with a blissful feeling of happiness like I have never felt on the earth.

All my worries of life, for a moment became non-existent, and it was a precious time, with my guide as he was guiding me over the house and fields below. We slowly began to descend, Running Deer was clearly taking me somewhere in the Spirit World, but I didn't know where. We gently came to a landing and I was standing in front of a house I hadn't been to before.

This house wasn't over glamorous or like a mansion, but more a humble home with a warm feeling, it appeared to be made of 'bricks' and had the general features you would expect on a standard home on earth; windows, doors etc. The front garden had two grass lawns with a path in the centre leading to the front door, and the lawns had the most gorgeous flower boarders, and again the colours are so bright, vibrant and more healthy looking. The boarders contained red and pink Roses, Sunflowers, Tulips and many other beautiful colourful flowers.

As I am standing looking at the house I said to Running Deer "Where are we? Whose house is this?" To my guides response "Go in and find out, don't worry it will be ok." Hmmmm, I know YOUR idea of ok is, it normally means you throw me in the deep end, so what you up to this time? I thought to myself.

I very suddenly got the idea my guide wasn't following me into the house, as I got closer to the door I could hear loud music, very loud in fact. The music began to become familiar to me, I began to realise I could hear Elvis Presley being played.

I walked into the house and shouted "Hello." I looked around the room I was in, it seemed to me like the Living Room, there was furniture, well organised, with photos on the wall. I didn't recognise the people in the photos I was looking at, and I was getting more confused, as I kept looking round for clues, trying to work out who could possibly be living here. It was like being part of an episode of 'Through the Keyhole' with Lloyd Grossman and I was rubbish at that too.

The music was deafening as one song finished and then began playing another 'Can't help falling in love'. I became aware I was no longer alone in the house, as I am still in the living-room; I look over towards the far left corner of the room where there is a corridor or hallway.

As I looked over, a man walked in the room very casual as if they were expecting me. "Alright Spence." I heard in my mind. "Richard? Is this place yours?" I replied back to him. "I should have guessed with the Elvis music playing, it was your place." I remember starting to laugh as I was still trying to take in my experience.

As I looked at Richard his appearance was the same as the last time I saw him on the earth. His hair was brushed back, he still had his sideburns and he was wearing a blue long sleeved shirt and black trousers. I asked Richard how he got the house. "This is the house I always wanted." He told me. "I can have everything I want here where I am, watch." Richard confirmed in my mind and then he reached out his hand and a beer appeared instantly, and he casually sipped from the glass of a cold pint of his favourite tipple.

I was a little stunned to say the least with what I just witnessed in my 'minds' eye, as I am visiting this vast spiritual place of dreams, where everything you desire just manifests before your very eyes so to speak. If Richard wanted a pint of his favourite lager, or a cigarette it manifests as soon as he thinks of it. "What car are you driving? I asked in my mind. "I don't need one, what's the point of driving to a place when you can just think of it and be there instantaneously." Richard continued "You can have a car if you want the experience of cruising down a country lane, surrounded by animals and endless fields if you want to." "You can have a convertible and feel the wind in your face and through your hair, but only if you want to. It's your choice if it's your hearts' desire, so be it." Richard confirmed.

Then within an instant, Richard and myself were in a new place, what I can only describe as a 'cinema room'. This is where he learnt about things to do with his life in regards to the lessons of his soul. I looked around the room and I could see beautiful pillars sticking out from the walls with flowers carved into them, and the walls in between were a deep burgundy red colour with various old paintings on them.

The room was gently lit-up by small wall lights, there were rows of very comfy seats and at the front of the room there was a large cinema screen. "What's this place? Are we watching a film that ain't released yet?" I asked Richard, to which he laughed and replied "No this is where I came to gain further understanding about my thoughts and actions whilst I was on the earth, we all have to go through this, even you." "Will I experience this then when I return to spirit?" I asked Richard. "Not necessarily in the same environment, but you will have to go through a similar processes of learning."

The lights on the walls began to dim suddenly as the screen came on at the front of the room. We both sat in a seat and began watching the screen. It began to play a snippet of a memory from a random evening of Richard and I in his house before he passed. It was of us laughing and sharing jokes, it was explained to me, that what was being shown on the screen, was for me to learn. Everything that happens over time is recorded and stored within the consciousness of the universe called the Akashic Records. The Akashic Records, record every thought, feeling, action, and everything that has ever happened, from the beginning of time, the spirit world is limitless; it goes beyond all concepts of the human mind to the point most of us in this world won't comprehend.

Where Richard had taken me was to a realm of learning where we all go to. This is for the purpose of our own souls' further understanding of what it experienced, through how each of us, as an individual chose to live our own life. Richard explained when he watched back the various parts of his life, he needed to, understood each situation in life is a test for the soul, no one fails, they just gather further understanding of truth. Each situation he watched back gave him a clearer understanding of how his words, thoughts and actions created the outcomes he didn't want.

I was told as we go through life facing day to day situations that test the soul, allowing it to gather further understanding of how each life lesson can be handled. Each person you meet in your life is part of your soul group, you have known them long before the present life you are living in now, and they are either a reflection of you, or a teacher to you. You have had connections to them through many, many previous lifetimes, and you are put together to learn from each other. We have to learn how to get along with each other. Each situation will teach you about personal responsibility, love, truth, hate, hurt, appreciation, happiness, sadness, deceit, jealousy, gratitude, anger, and joy just to name a few.

How we deal with each person or situation we face will determine either good or bad karma, in which we are constantly creating depending on how we choose to approach each life situation, person or any living thing. Over time the soul needs to understand many lessons, one lesson for so many of us is how to approach many of these situations in life, with unconditional love, and free of ignorance.

When we are born into this world we are all here with particular 'conditions' that are connected to the soul, and these elements of the soul will be faced, and need work on, and healing. These areas are to do with the many elements to life situations, and various forms of relationships that have happened in our past lives that have not been healed, or fully understood yet. These facets are tests or lessons for our souls growth and are part of our personal karma I was told. How we lived our previous life can bring certain 'conditions' of the soul forward into the present on this earth realm, in order for each of us to grow and gain further understanding through the tests of life.

The 'conditions' are related to the vast array of life situations you have to encounter, for the soul to understand. Each is a specific lesson in order to heal and grow from, if this lesson is not learnt the cycle will repeat itself. For instance one of your lessons could be to do with a 'type' of partner you have/had in your life, where you go through various moments in your life, to the understanding of lessons, of different forms of relationships, good and bad. If we notice the same specific past problem keeps arising in new relationships, then that lesson has not yet been learnt or addressed. Therefore it will be repeated until we, as an individual address it, understand why it happened, learn from it, grow from it and heal from that relationship lesson. During the time we are here on earth, if various lessons have not been completed or fully understood, they can result in us reincarnating back to earth, and this cycle will also repeat just like our repeated cycles/lessons in our physical lives now. Therefore you stay within the constructs of this limited reality, your soul will not progress and it cannot move beyond this point, until the 'you' in the physical lifetime, chooses to lift the veil that is blinding you and holding your souls progression back, so 'you' can set your 'soul self' free to venture into the higher realms of understanding of truth.

These conditions of the soul are also connected to previous lives, through good and bad karma we have created through the lives we have lived, and by the way we have chosen to live them. People that create bad karma over their lifetime/s will face a true reflection of their thoughts, words and actions that have been brought upon by themselves, through past lives, and past connections to the people in your soul group and brought into your current life reality now. This is based upon the types of situations and life lessons created, due to their own choices of what reflects their personal karma.

The same applies to those who go out their way to help others and create good karma; what you put out to the universe you get back. Hence we all must do our best and pay attention in regards to our thoughts and actions towards others, at all times. After Richard told me this, he ended with "No one escapes karma."

When Richard said that I felt Running Deer drawing close and I began to get a feeling my visit was coming to an end. Very quickly I was back in the living room of Richards' house; the sun was coming through the living room window, and gently lit the room up in a golden glow. I could see the sunlight peeking through the fine gap in the front door as I said my goodbyes to Richard and walked out his door. I was then gently guided back out of the meditation.

I have learnt over the years that having a strong bond with my guides is paramount, over time you learn to trust them that is why they are there. The two experiences were very unique from each other, but both were parts of my journey I shall never forget.

That is the beauty with working with spirit and developing your spirituality, each experience will be as beautiful as the last, and you will build precious memories with your guides and spirits over the years. Every experience I have had with spirit, are things in my life I am very much grateful for, a path of spirituality isn't an easy one, but it has endless blessings.

Chapter 6
My first Public Demonstration

*I*t's November 2003, and now I have been approximately developing at Parkside Spiritualist church for 4 years. At this point I had been sitting in development circles 3 times a week, various workshops at other churches like Villiers Street in Coventry. I had also been to the Arthur Findley college and working on myself at home.

The particular development circle I was sitting in was preparing the students for what they called "Presidency Day." What was meant by this day was, for the 7 selected students to be given the chance to hold a service together between them.

For the next commencing weeks leading up to the event, we were given more time on preparing ourselves for the service, fine tuning ourselves, and working on getting rid of certain habits, such as give your information from spirit as a statement, rather than asking questions.

For example, whilst working from platform it doesn't give the congregation much confidence when a medium says "I have got to come to you, is your mum in spirit? And is it her that passed from pneumonia?" What the medium should be saying is. "I know I need to speak to you, as I have your mother with me, from the world of spirit, and I am made aware she passed with pneumonia …."

It's very important as mediums to speak with conviction and a knowing of what they are receiving is truth, it is quite easy to slip into the trap of asking a question instead of giving it as a statement.

Believe me, there have been times on my own path over the past 20 years, doubt crept in, and I asked a question. I am conscious I have done it on occasions in the past, and it is only down to me to address it, and this should apply to all mediums.

When we ask questions, it makes the congregation or the person you are talking to, doubt that we have a spirit link at all. The truth is, if the medium has a strong link with the spirit communicator there shouldn't be any doubt present, as the consciousness of the spirit communicator is.

When we make the link with spirit we become aware of the many feelings and sensations the spirit world is expressing upon us. This way of delivery is only accomplished through dedicated development, total trust and confidence in spirit, your guides and yourself.

When we were practicing the scenarios of our roles that we will do during the service, these exercises were to understand delivery of prayer, philosophy, and working on our delivery of evidence and relaying a message; passing the information on as statements, not questions. The exercises were done from the church platform; this is so we could get an idea of what it's like prior to the day, and hopefully be prepared enough.

The day finally came, and I had been battling with nerves for the big day for around 2 or 3 days leading up to it. Although no one likes feeling nervous, it's a good sign. It shows you have a level head and you are humble, another positive element about nervous energy is, spirit works with the energy that is created within your stomach and around your Solar Plexus chakra.

The Solar Plexus chakra is a vital energy receptor whilst working with mediumship. This is because we pass and receive energy and frequency through this centre, and when used correctly, it will be your guide during a service, to point you in the right direction to the recipient, who the message is for.

When connecting with spirit and you are talking to the wrong person and you do not receive a verbal note, you can feel it. You are talking to the correct person by the feeling within the stomach area. This area is where you are notified of your inner tuition or intuition; when these unsettling feelings are present, that is your inner knowing, warning you that you are talking to the wrong soul.

Your intuition can also help you through your daily life if you take note of the sudden change in feelings. If something does not feel right, then it isn't, and this situation or place should be avoided.

I got myself ready, dressed in a black suit, white shirt and a light amethyst tie. My mother drove me to the church, as I didn't drive, and I still currently don't due to my eyesight, but I am working on that through positive manifestation.

We arrived at the church around half an hour prior to the start of the service, and thankfully before anybody arrived. Arriving early before doing a service I have found is very important, this time in a private room is the final opportunity to clear your mind and blend with your spirit team so you know you are completely ready to work. I have found the more dedication you put in to your development, the easier it can make our journey.

The other students arrived, and we discussed the order we were going to work in, once we were clear of how the order of service was working, this gave me some time to sit with my guide for around 20 minutes, bearing in mind I have also sat and meditated that morning for 30 to 45 minutes prior to leaving my home.

We were told there was an audience of around 135 people in the church, plus I knew some friends and family were planning to come and watch me work, and that's when the nerves really kicked in, but I knew I couldn't back out.

A gentle shiver came over me, as we were introduced to the audience whilst sitting on the church rostrum; it is always a good sign to let you know spirit are with you. The service started with everybody singing, and we sang something like 'Morning has broken'.

A lady from the group did the open prayer, followed by another song, and then a short philosophy was given by another student.

Once all the songs were done and the philosophy was addressed, it was time for the demonstration of mediumship. I wasn't first, but weather that's a good thing or a bad thing; take your pick the nerves are still going to be there.

With my development I have been trained to make sure we push our energy and awareness to the back of the room, in my opinion if you start from the back you know your energy is strong and you are present in your own power with spirit. Through my experience sometimes going to the first row, on my first link, I have found it to be more difficult and the energy and messages don't seem to flow the same.

What you tend to find at times, a minority of those that sit on the front two rows can be, as we say 'Message Grabbers'. These are the people you need your wits about you, because you can potentially give the wrong person a message, and they will accept it, even if they don't understand any of the message, they will say 'Yes' and take any information they can. This can be allowed to happen, for lessons for the medium, and the person deliberately taking someone else's message.

Previously mentioned, working with your Solar Plexus properly, this will allow you to realise you are talking to the right person or not. This is because spirit can send you a vibrational signal that will give you the feeling something is wrong. This is when you can confirm with the loved one in spirit you are speaking to the wrong person and you send out your energy again and see where you are drawn.

Once the appropriate link is established, and you have connected to the right person, then you will feel a pull in your Solar Plexus, which will give you the feeling of the right direction, and the right person who can take all the information provided by the medium.

After a couple of the other students passed on their messages and got validation of their links from the congregation, the wait, that felt like it had no end, finally was over, and it was now my turn to see if I could actually put what I have learnt over the past couple of years to real practice.

As it was my turn to stand up I leant forward to stand, and as I was looking down I closed my eyes for a moment and in my mind I said "Spirit I need you." I stood up and glanced around the room just to take everything in. I noticed my late uncle David and his wife aunty Gwen on the front row, as I'm facing the audience to my right.

My guide Running Deer began to draw close and give me a feeling of calmness, this allowed me to clear my mind and focus, I sent my intentions to push out my aura, to overlap the congregation and raise my awareness, patiently waiting for the first link to connect with me.

I started to scan the room and looking towards various areas of the audience, until I felt a stronger pull from my solar plexus towards the right direction and a person. The person I linked in with was a lady at the far left corner, at the back of the hall.

Now like I have mentioned, I have a visual impairment and this means I can only see faces of people in front of me reasonably clear up to around 15 to 20 feet away. Or to put it another way if you were standing on the other side of the road I wouldn't recognise you, because details beyond that point on people's faces become unclear, and I cannot read certain facial details or expressions, but this does not stop me from living a normal life, I can get around ok.

For that reason, for a long while it was the main reason of my nerves, because I knew I had a physical limitation to my sight, and I was always worried I wouldn't be able to locate the person in the room with my own eyes, and for a while, I hid this information for numerous years from the public.

From here it should be clearer to you why I rely solely on my guidance from my solar plexus for guiding me to people. With frequency the majority of the time you can't see it, so in time I stopped worrying about what I cannot see because my spirit team taught me that frequency does not lie.

As I looked to the back of the room to make sure I was with the right person, my guide locked my head towards the desired person the spirit world wished me to speak to. "May I come to the lady right at the back of the room in the left hand corner?" I announced.
"Yes" the woman replied with a bit of surprise to her voice and a little stunned that she had been chosen.

"I have a gentleman with me from the world of spirit, and I am aware that he is your grandfather on your fathers' side of the family." I said to her. "Yes" the lady confirmed. "He gives me the name George and I know he was shot in the left leg during the Second World War, because I can feel it within the area of my knee, and I know that your grandfather died with some shards of the bullet still present in the knee, as they couldn't be removed." I explained.

The lady gasped for a moment and confirmed "yes that's definitely my grandfather George." I went on to say "Your grandfather is telling me in your living room, he has seen a broken angel figurine that is placed at the centre on the middle shelf, in the display cabinet you have, and he confirms to me it is the right wing on the angel that is damaged." Again she confirmed it to be true.

For a moment I nervously giggled, because I was stunned that she could take this information and I cannot see the face of the person I am talking to, neither can I see their mouth move. I just hear the lady's voice travel back to me, from the direction I am looking.

I began to describe the grandfather further. "I know your grandfather is taller than me, around 5ft. 10 with salt and pepper hair, slim build, and his personality, although he came forward firm and regimented, he also had a very witty side." "Yes he did" the lady said. I continued "He just told me you didn't drop the Christmas cake this year." The woman laughed loudly along with the congregation, perked-up with a quick reply, whilst still chuckling to herself. "No that was last year Spencer."

Her response then made me laugh, which broke my concentration for a moment and I had to compose myself again. Running Deer is a guide that is rather firm and he doesn't really have a sense of humour. It's his personality I can feel at times when I have to become serious again, he reigns me back in, and helps me become more focused and removes distractions.

I settled back into the link quite quickly, and got serious again as I began to feel a new energy making a connection to me. It was a very young child; I became aware of the energy drawing in close from my left hand side.

I looked towards the direction I felt the energy coming from; although I couldn't see it, I knew it felt around 3ft tall. I continued on and told the woman I was aware of a young boy, and I felt the child passed over at around the age of 3 or 4 years old, from Leukaemia.

The energy in the room filled with emotion as the toddler came forward, the congregation reacts with empathy, and I could hear someone say "Oh bless him." Before I could clarify the relation of this child to the lady, she announced it was her son, and he sadly passed before his fourth birthday.

I passed on a message to the lady from her son; to say this was a challenge was an understatement. Children are one of the hardest and most challenging situations, as a medium to face. It doesn't necessarily get easier; we just learn to cope with it better. You have to learn to emotionally detach, but at the same time, be compassionate, kind and still come from unconditional love, and think before you speak. You don't want to make their grief any worse; they are there to get strength and comfort from you, and that comes with a huge responsibility.

I finished off the message for the lady, and turned to the next student to acknowledge it was their turn. The student I turned to had previously given a message but it became very apparent nerves got the better of them, and I could fully understand, so I looked at other students who wished to follow on and do the last few minutes of the service.

It suddenly dawned on me no one else was willing to continue, bear in mind it was our first time for all 7 of us, and briefly there was a moment of panic on the platform, I guess everybody got hit with 'stage fright'. The chairperson whispered to me "Can you continue? There is only time for one more message."

I looked around the room glancing at the audience, and thankfully another link made contact with me, so I turned to the chairperson, and gave her a nod to let her know I was continuing.

A lady with red hair was sitting in the front row, and I only remember bringing an animal through for her. I asked the lady may I speak to her, and she responded "Yes of course."

I closed my eyes for a moment because my heart was racing, my nerves were really strong. This was because my uncle Dave was in my sights now as I moved to the other end of the rostrum, and at times family and friends add unnecessary pressure that is brought on by our own self.

I quickly glanced at my uncle Dave and my aunty Gwen and gave them a smile to acknowledge them both, and turned back to the lady to continue her message. I said to her "I have a dog that has made a connection with me, and I can see it is a German shepherd.

I cannot precisely remember the dog's name I gave but in the back of my mind as I am writing, I keep hearing Cassie, so I will use that name for the purpose of the book.
I told the lady I knew it was her dog and they had a very powerful spiritual bond, the dog was very loving in nature, but highly protective of you. "Yes she was." the lady confirmed.

I am aware as I connect with your dog; I know it had problems in its back legs, because my legs are hurting." I explained to the woman on the front row. I then told her I know it's the back legs, as when spirit brings through four legged animals, my legs refer to the hind legs, and my arms always refer to the front legs. As I explained this, it created a couple of giggles from the audience, I also laughed at the way I described it to, but looking at it, it's very logical.

I heard the words gently come from behind me from the chairperson, "You are called to time Spencer." I then brought the message to a close, and thanked the lady for working with me, and returned to my seat.

The chairperson then addressed the members of the audience that the service had finished, and asked a fellow student to close the service in prayer. The church went silent as the only voice you could hear was the soft tone of the medium saying the closing prayer. It brought stillness to me, my heart began to slow down and return to normal, as now the nerves subsided, I actually got through it I thought, and a great feeling of relief washed over me.

The audience was told there was tea/coffee available for those who wish to stop and chat, the chairperson then said "let us give these brave students a big round of applause." I remember dipping my head, as I began to smile to myself and felt sheepish and trying to hide in my chair. I cannot take compliments when I work for spirit, I can't accept them, but that's who I am, and it has never changed in 20 years. Messages come through us, not from us. The true credit should be given to the universe. But that's my personal opinion.

I then saw my uncle stand up clapping loudly, encouraging everybody else to stand with him and do the same. The whole church stood up with him, and there was at least what felt like a minute or two of applause.

Once the service was finished we left the platform to speak to our friends and family, as it was now time to relax. My uncle David was the first person to greet me off the rostrum, right hand stretched out as he walked proudly towards me, with perfect posture, shoulders back, with his head held high.
He looked right into my eyes and said "I am highly proud of you today son." as we shook hands with his firm grip of authority, whilst placing his left hand on my right shoulder. When my uncle Dave shook your hand, he meant it.

It was his way of saying you have gained his respect. He was ex-military for the Royal British Legion Standard Bearers, and an Army boxing champion. A true gent, he was a man that had integrity, honour and was highly respected by those who knew him. And a damn good ballroom dancer, with his wife Gwen may I add.

I giggled very childlike, as he complemented me. "Son I don't understand what you did today, and I don't know how you did it, but that was amazing." He said to me. I began to feel the emotion within me come up into my throat, I quickly swallowed. "Thank you." I replied clearing my throat, and removing a single tear from the corner of my eye.

The roles had become reversed, one moment ago; I was standing and talking to people and giving them hope, and acting with compassion and a responsibility in a position of leadership. Now I am being humbled by a man that knows, and truly understands, the meaning of leadership. I have once again become the student, listening to a teacher of life.

He continued. "The bit I liked was how you described the problems of the legs with the dog. Your legs are the back legs, and your arms are the front legs." My uncle Dave then concluded. "That made me chuckle, but it makes perfect sense to me."

We continued to chat for a few moments and spoke to my aunty Gwen. The compliments paused for a moment when one of my school friends, who I spent a lot of time with, came up to me smiling. My aunty and uncle then mingled amongst others and spoke to my mum.

My friend Craig was a sceptic and I wasn't expecting him to be instantly convinced. As we hung around together during my development, like him and many friends, and family, ribbed me about what I did and still do now, but that's their personal point of understanding and awareness.

Since the passing of my mum in 2011 there isn't really any family that believe in what I do, but I carry on. You can give them all the proof in the world, but they won't believe any of it until they choose to. You don't have to try and prove anything to anybody; they have to prove you wrong. Your path is your truth nobody else's and their path is their truth.

We shook hands and said our usual hellos; I asked him how he felt about what I did. Craig replied "Bit vague wern' it? "Vague?" I said as I laughed off the comment. To my response was "You are entitled to your opinion, but I think those two ladies I spoke to, may tell you different." At that point my mother saw Craig and came over to him, gave him a hug and a kiss on his cheek. I would say that was a divinely timed distraction.

I managed to speak to the ladies that I gave messages to, and I found out it was the first time the little boy ever came through. That moment is priceless to both of us, and it was a huge privilege to me that the soul chose that instant to come forward, and the first link of a loved one is always special for the one receiving the message.

Over the past 20 years I have learnt on the path of mediumship, you are going to face many moments of highs and lows. There are going to be times people praise you and there are going to be times people will use hurtful words towards you. You will learn to take the rough with the smooth, and you will learn to truly appreciate all that life allows you to face.

Truly embellish every moment the universe and spirit bless you with, because those moments will give you the strength to get through the challenging sceptics. They will challenge you regardless of the evidence you give. I've given friends readings that are sceptic and told them things I knew nothing about, but they still continue to deny it, even after specific details.

If they deny it, it is irrelevant to your path or your spiritual progress, it doesn't mean you gave the wrong information, it's just the wrong time for them to receive it, but a seed has been planted.

If you know within your heart your intentions came from a place of unconditional love and truth, and you are aligned to natural law, it doesn't matter what they think of what you do, because in your heart you will feel it was the truth.

Their ignorance and denial does not affect your journey, we are all independently living and resonating on our own level of consciousness of understanding and what we focus on affects the level of our awareness and understanding of things.
Don't allow sceptics or anybody who chooses to be negative towards you to pull you down, that is a reflection of their ignorance. Doing that is giving away your power, do not bow down and lower your worth to please them. We are all here for the purpose of self-growth, and to provide service for the greater good of humanity.

Learn to understand the true value of your soul.
As you strive forward on your own path you will gather more understanding, things that don't make sense to you now, will make sense in the near future. Things that don't resonate to be your 'Truth' in this

book may do one day, or it may not, it all depends on how your journey pans out. The universe guided you this far, and the universe will also guide those that are not so enlightened.

We are here on Earth constantly living in the present to gather more understanding. This planet is a simulator for the growth of the soul, and we are here to find out and understand what we truly are, and what our life's purpose is. Most of us started as a sceptic on this path, if not all, but something opened our minds and brought us to this point of awareness and understanding.

There is no such thing as coincidence that is simply synchronicity and signs of guidance from the universe. Every piece of your life puzzle fits into place at the right time, as and when we have gathered enough understanding for that piece to fit.

You cannot force truth on anybody; it's down to us all individually to consent to receiving and accepting the truth when we are faced with it. Those that are sceptical will be awakened by the universal consciousness eventually.

The pieces of your puzzle of life to name just a few are; people, situations and knowledge you gather through your daily life. Those people and situations point you to knowledge, and that knowledge points you to a new level of awareness, and clarity of understanding.

The truth is we are all energy, and energy cannot die, we don't die, we only change form. We all are energy and frequency, and that truth cannot be changed regardless of who chooses to accept it or not.

Right up to this moment your existence has been living eternally; your living Being/Soul/Light Body has been around longer than you may be able to comprehend right now.

We are told by scientists our universe is around 13.8 billion years old, although a 'true' number, without relevant knowledge, would be very difficult to put an exact number on it. This is what scientists have concluded upon, through their years of research and tests, through the evidence they have found and provided us with.

From my understanding that's what is recorded as physical matter, NOT consciousness, energy, vibration or frequency. From my point of awareness, I cannot give you a precise number of years either, but what I would personally say, the age of the universe is definitely considerably older, and working out the time you have existed for, would also be a very complex answer, but your existence will also older than this earth itself.

The only way for all the truth to be revealed about the creation of the universe is through us communicating with the universe/spirit itself. By combining spirituality with science, then and only then, will truthful and evidential research provide proof of creation and consciousness? But I can't see that happening at any time soon, because it would cause a religious uproar across the world.

For this to actually be successful, all man's ideologies, religious beliefs and any intention of corruption must be removed from those in the scientific field that will carry out the research. This rule must also apply to the mediums that would be used as vessels for channelling this information.

All tests that are carried out must be from an unbiased point of awareness of the scientists, and mediums. All tests necessary must be carried out through the strict instruction from spiritual teachers that have had many years' experience with Trance Mediumship, and or Physical Mediumship who give clear understanding of how trance and physical mediumship works. The appropriate teacher/moderator will be assigned to each test in accordance with which test is performed.

From the point of research for science, they would have to follow instruction from the spiritual teachers from those in the specific field Trance/Physical Mediumship, to give them a basis of understanding of how the spirit world and trance mediumship works.

The medium used must also follow the strict instructions such as; a safe and controlled environment for the medium, for all tests. This is **paramount**.

Once the trance or physical mediumship sessions begin, it would then be down to us listening and witnessing what the universe wants us to know as truth. From creation, to fully understanding the true mechanics of the universe and consciousness, ourselves, and providing true evidence of spirit, that will not be ridiculed or ignored.

Chapter 7
The start to my
Journey of Trance
Mediumship

The last chapter leads me up nicely to the next poignant part of my development. I have been developing my mediumship now for around 6 years at this point. Through my development I met a very special lady whilst sitting in her home circle, and her name was Pauline, who gained her angel wings March 2015.

This beautiful soul guided me up until the point, where I helped her towards her final moments battling cancer. I began sitting in a private circle run by Pauline, I was part of that group for a number of years, prior to running our own joint circle together years later.

Originally the group was for the general mechanics of mediumship, using Clairvoyance, Clairsentience and Clairaudience. Over a period of time Pauline held guided meditations, and this gave my Native American guide Running Deer the opportunity to introduce himself, and speak through me in trance, to the rest of the group.

Pauline or 'Polly' of which many people will remember her as, encouraged these opportunities of trance, in return to further my own development of my mediumship. This was the wonderful thing about Polly, when you sat in her home circle as long as you were acting in total respect and unconditional love, she would allow you to explore all areas of your development, and many others have said the same.

The meditations helped me relax enough to move my conscious mind away, which in turn allows my guide to come forward and speak, inspiring and intellectual forms of truth information.

Over a period of time your point of awareness changes, at the beginning you are building a bond and learning to blend with your guide, and being dedicated to sit. This over time allows Overshadowing of the medium to happen, into light states of trance to developing a deeper state of trance mediumship over time.

In order to enable trance mediumship you must work under the principle of trance control, to enable a communicator from spirit to regulate the medium's mind and body, allowing the medium to speak.

This is performed when the medium's mind is completely settled and rested, and witnessing such a magnificent spiritual experience is a blessing. Once the medium's mind is in this deep rested state, this allows the spirit communicator to develop a more powerful connection with the medium's aura, and subconscious mind, creating a very strong bond.

There are many different degrees of trance, and at this point I was being overshadowed by my guide, but do not get this confused with trance. Overshadowing is a form of your development that is the building blocks of a bond between the medium and a guide, then creating the development of trance, leading up to full trance communicator control.

Overshadowing can happen during your meditation at a point within your development, where you have established a powerful and strong relationship with your guide/s, allowing them to blend with your aura. Aspects of the guide's personality come forward and are expressed upon the medium, giving them certain feelings.

When the blend with the aura is accomplished the feelings can include; a feeling of being larger in build, but this doesn't affect the physical appearance of your body. You can feel expressions of their origin; Native American, Egyptian or Mandarin for example. You can feel their personality; having a feeling of sternness, a serious outlook or they can be much gentler and have a much calmer personality.

You can feel if they are coming forward as male or female, you may become aware of 'words' coming into your mind, and feeling encouraged saying them.

These are just some expressions and feelings to expect when you are sitting with your guides yourself.

The process of this development cannot be forced, take your time, it's neither a race, nor a competition, it can only be encouraged by the right experienced people, you cannot be 'taught' to do trance, it's an ability within some mediums that has to be encouraged with help by experienced sitters, or through development with your own guides over a period of time. Once the spirit world knows you are committed to sit, they will help it flourish.

You need to be aware that not all mediums are able to sit for trance mediumship and unfortunately this can open a door to fraud from a minority that can't do it, but so badly want to. When mediums attempt these untruthful acts, the information you will hear from 'that' medium will only be words coming from their own ego and human mind.

When my Native guide first began to overshadow me, I would feel a lot larger in build, Running Deer expresses himself over 6 ft. 7 inches tall, and I am only physically 5 ft. 3 ½ inches tall.

At the beginning it felt as if he was squeezing himself into my smaller framed body, but remember it's only an expression/feeling of his energy being placed over mine. Spirit does not actually get inside your 'Physical' body but rather blend within your aura that is part of your etheric body.

As I blend with my guide, my posture would change very strongly, I would become much more upright, and my head would be held high, as his dominating personality comes forward and places the feeling of his personality over mine.

At first it started with a few words of encouragement for the group to enable their growth, then more started to come forward; short verses of philosophy and then for much longer 15 to 20 minutes or so. Over time the blend became stronger, but the feelings of my guide's energy squeezing into my body subsided over a period of a couple of months.

After a few months of my Native speaking to the group weekly, one particular occasion Polly became aware of a new energy coming around me, and told me it is a new guide. This guide is more relaxed, and is of Mandarin origin.

The Mandarin guide has a very different form of delivery, much softer approach to situations, with a gentle sense of humour, but still carries vast wisdom. Running Deer has a more abrupt and firm delivery, a stance of authority, but I will talk more about him in another part of this book.

The new energy that Polly felt had made themselves known during a meditation, he didn't make contact with me first, he approached Pauline and explained to her who he was, and who he was for. The guide entered the circle this way, in a form of showing respect to the teacher, and he knew he needed permission to access the group.

This kind of thing happening isn't, in my opinion, unusual, as whilst teaching I have had the same experiences. As and when your guides introduce themselves to you, this choice is based on the free will of that guide, and they know when is the best time to introduce themselves to you and how.

Guides can and will introduce themselves to you in meditation of course, as well, but it was on this occasion he decided to come via the teacher, of which he knew I highly respected and trusted.

Pauline addressed to me that a new guide wants to connect with me whilst I was still meditating; I ran this past my guide Running Deer, as he is my 'controller' or 'Overseer.' For many years in my early development I ran everything to do with my spiritual path through him, that's why they are there.

It was confirmed the new contact was going to be a part of my spirit team/guides. Now in the present, this guide named Chow Li is the main one who speaks through me in my trance sittings, because of his subtle and gentle approach, people click with him.

During the circle with Pauline, Chow Li began blending with me through her guidance. When he blends with me I shrink down in the chair and become hunched up, he is around 4 ft. 6 inches tall, this is how he chooses to blend with me. When I am getting closer to speak, I become more upright in the chair my head raises with a smile and then I speak when I feel encouraged to.

It was his soft voice flowing with words of enlightenment that came through to the group on a much more regular basis than Running Deer. The others of the group and Pauline took a shine to his tranquil approach to the teaching of life. Although he is a very gentle soul that comes forward he can still be firm if he needs to be, but generally that isn't his style.

The development group was held on a Sunday afternoon, but this Sunday Chow Li felt he needed to give a member of the group a message. We had all done a meditation, guided as usual by Polly, and we always gave feedback of what happened during our meditations, so we could be given some insight into what certain things meant and gather further understanding about ones own progression.

One particular member of the group was talking about their meditation, and gave a description of what happened. The person said they saw themselves riding quite fast on their motorbike, and they also saw their "Guardian Angel" as the student put it; flying behind them trying to keep up, the person began to giggle and found what they saw rather amusing.

I turned to them and said "It could be the spirit world telling you to slow down, and you shouldn't ride faster than your angel can fly." I explained. The student laughed it off again, and their partner mentioned that the member in the group does ride on their motorbike too fast, and should slow down and listen.

I told them the universe gives you everything for a reason, again reluctantly taking any notice, Polly told the student just to be careful, and then the attention was turned to another student talking about their meditation and how they did.

Pauline paired the group for a little while to do mini readings, and to help gain more practice of various areas of mental mediumship, using our tools such as clairvoyance and clairaudience. Once we did the mini readings we all sat together again and discussed how we did.

Whilst the others were talking, it started to become clear Chow Li wanted to speak to the group, and let's say he was being a little more eager and pushy on this occasion. I made Pauline and the group aware he wanted to speak, but I was unaware as to why.

I made myself comfortable and proceeded to prepare the blending process with Chow Li, as the group were sitting around me I closed my eyes. My mind started to become quieter, and I set my intention of trance mediumship to happen with my guide.

As I am sitting I can feel his energy begin to come closer behind me. I scratch the back of my head and rub my face for a couple of moments, as I start reacting to the energy as it blends effortlessly within my aura.

As Chow Li continues to blend, I feel myself going into a deeper state of consciousness. As I blend with spirit my conscious mind activity slows down, allowing that part of the mind to become dormant and my guide to take a form of control of my voice box, and this allows the communicator to speak, and this will create the voice of the medium to also change completely.

There are many degrees of trance communication – from a light overshadowing of the medium, to a deep trance, or full control by the spirit communicator. On this occasion I was taken much deeper than normal which means I don't recall what I specifically said.

This is quite normal with trance, due to different degrees of trance, it will depend on the experience you have. You could be aware of the words entering your mind and you speak them in a very light state, or they can take you much deeper.

When you allow yourself to go deeper this alters the state of the medium's brain, and lowers the frequency into a theta/ delta state which is in the range of 4 to 7 Hz and changing the state of consciousness of the medium. This is what causes the 'memory loss due to the medium's conscious mind being temporary supressed, but at times you can get snippets of flashbacks to your conscious mind afterwards, of small pieces of information that the communicator said.

Whilst the medium is sitting for trance, they must speed up their frequency, and the spirit communicator must slow theirs down. When this happens it creates a mutual ground for communication to link and develop.

As the deeper state is present, and the medium's conscious mind is moved 'out the way', the voice, mannerisms, facial expressions, personality and voice will be that of the spirit communicator, whilst the medium is in the deep state, or under full trance control.

There are other aspects to be aware of whilst working with Trance Mediumship. Trance creates physical effects on the body – for example, the heart rate of the medium slows down, and so does the breathing of the medium also. This also creates the altering of the mediums body temperature to drop and also creates a difference in the mediums vibration on a cellular level. All of which will be made evident during the temporary suppression of the mediums conscious mind.

The following information was fed back to me and there will not be any information given of the person's identity, whilst describing my experience. The information I am providing is just for giving the reader an insight and an example of what can happen and what information at times can be provided in the right circumstances during a trance mediumship sitting.

I felt myself go a lot deeper than normal, it was very different, because I was used to having some awareness, but this time it was "lights out" so to speak. I remember Pauline talking me through very gently and quietly, and the last I remember hearing was "Just go with it…"

The length of time I was talking for is very unclear to me, once I heard the last few words that Polly said, there was a void, a moment of "nothing" but still existing, still living and vibrating. It took me a couple of minutes to start but once the blend was completed it became apparent to the group that my whole personality changed, and the way I sat was also very different.

I was told that when the guide was speaking, he was very expressive with my hands, as some of us do in a general conversation. The voice was very subtle and flowed with a gentle touch of "Poshness."

Chow Li speaks with an etiquette that draws people in. He has a very polite teasing sense of humour, for instance on many occasions when people say "May I ask a question?" he has been known to reply "You may ask, but it doesn't mean I will give you an answer." then chuckles to himself whilst explaining his sense of humour.

With trance you get to see many wonderful characters and personalities from the world of spirit, each of them are beautiful in their own unique way and it is a privilege to watch.

Chow Li addressed the group and thanked them for giving him the permission to speak. The spirit world will always show respect, if the mediums personal intentions on their path are pure, and aligned with Natural Law.

My guide gave each student some guidance on their spiritual path. The intentions for trance doesn't tend to tell people about their love life, its purpose is to empower us all through intellectual thought provoking conversation of truth, and not to stroke the human ego.

After speaking to the other members, Chow Li's attention was brought to one particular person in the group. According to the feedback I was informed my guide immediately raised the subject matter of the students' meditation and proceeded to talk about the symbolic meaning behind what they received.

Chow Li concluded to the specific person that, the spirit world had the intention of sending that person a warning about the way they pursue to ride their motorbike. I was also informed, in the feedback, that Chow Li gave them a very short summary of the near misses they previously had prior to this particular day.

The lack of respect from the student in response to what my guide told them was unexpected from the group, this resulting in another polite lecture on their attitude and behaviour towards spirit.

The spirit communicator that comes through a medium will not get into a "public argument" with you because the guide knows the level of awareness the person is at, that they are talking to. All that information is fed to the spirit communicator through vibration and frequency, which is the very basic mechanics of the conscious universe.

Again from my understanding during this trance session, my guide said something on the lines of. "Young 'Person' when the spirit world makes the effort to allow these moments of knowledge and truth to be shared to a group of souls, with a magnitude like those of you here today, comes with great pleasure for us to be allowed to share our views. But your level of ignorance leaves me to say these final words to you, before I vacate this instrument."

According to Pauline and the members of the group Chow Li's final words were. "The spirit world at times can pre-warn you of unnecessary harm, through our teachings and guidance that will bring those who listen to a greater understanding of truth. I have advised you of how to keep yourself safe; I would take heed of what I told you." He continued to say "Everything in life is about choices, what choice are you going to make?"

Before the student could give an answer Chow Li withdrawn himself and pulled away ending the session, eventually I opened my eyes looking at the person with an expression of 'I have been told off look' on their face.

The truth is the intention of the sitting was to allow the person to see their ways were not serving their purpose, and the universe was looking out for that person, and trying to protect them. As a result of the student not listening I had to receive the very sad news around a week later that the person was involved in an accident.

The student was speeding on their motorbike and took a corner too quickly hitting another car head on, as it was approaching the junction, and consequently putting them in hospital. It was first thought that the injuries were serious, but thankfully I was informed weeks later the person did make a full recovery, and I would like to think the universe gave that person a second chance.

It is vitally important whilst wanting to sit for trance that your intentions are 'set' with Natural Law, and Unconditional love. The reason being when you place yourself in the position to allow trance to happen, you are giving the spirit world permission to speak for you.

This takes huge trust, and you must have an understanding of trance mediumship, and set the correct intentions. The same pure intentions coinciding with Natural Law and Unconditional Love must also be applied to all other areas of your mediumship.

Chapter 8
Working with
Healing Energy

I have been involved with healing from the near beginning of my path, from having received healing for the first time, to also giving healing to many others over the years up to the present day. My path of healing started after developing for a few months.

It was suggested to me by my friend Marie who I worked with at the youth club, and she informed me, it may also do me some good. The healing at the time was held at Parkside Spiritualist Church, in Coventry. It was open to all walks of life with no discrimination, and it worked on a free will donation basis, those donations went towards the running of the church, and it was held on Wednesday afternoons at the time.

We got there around 1.50pm, as the door opened at 2pm. As we entered I noticed two rows of chairs. One row to the left of the church for people to sit, and wait, and on the right, several chairs were out for each healer that was available that afternoon, to do the healing of those who ever came along.

I remember sitting in a chair, once I was called up by a tall slim gentleman, in his mid-forty's. The man explained what he was going to do, and with my permission to rest his hands upon my shoulders and keeping them there throughout the healing session.
Whilst the hands of the healer are placed upon the sitters shoulders, the healing energy from the world of spirit passes through him and they shall receive the healing where needed within them.

I was told to close my eyes and relax and just go with the flow, and take myself to a place of peace and tranquillity, similar to you doing meditation, but you set your intention to receiving healing energy from the universe, via the healer.

Having some brief experience with meditation I rapidly began to go in to a very deep meditation, my body became weightless, tension from my neck and the top of my shoulders started to ease. A gentle warmth started to radiate from the gentleman's hands as the energy started to absorb within me soothing my mind, body and spirit.

Whilst my eyes were closed and the healing was in duration, I just let my mind go, like in the meditation meeting with my first guide, I was in a small boat gently gliding over some very light waves of an ocean. It was so calm, I could hear the waves of the water washing and brushing against the side of the boat, as they moved me forward rocking me gently like a loving protective mother would cradling a child.

The sky was so blue, the Suns golden rays of light were vibrantly shining and glistening down on me. I could feel the energy of the man's hands still working through me, but as I am looking at the blue sky in my mind, it's like the energy is coming from Sun and gently resonating through every fibre, every muscle, every vein, and every cell within my being.

It was pure bliss of complete blessedness and a heavenly and euphoric moment, at this point all my worries of life just disappeared from my thoughts and feelings. As I continued moving forwards, the boat was being guiding effortlessly gently rocking and swaying side to side, as it cuts through the waves like a hot knife through butter.

As I was being guided I could see a range of mountains in the distance as they began to become clearer into my focus. There was not another boat or cruise liner in sight. It was just me, the ocean, a beautiful blue sky, and the essence of the healing energy emanating, and calmly absorbing into me.

I was heading straight towards the mountains, the boat picked up speed, but the motion of the boat didn't change, it was still gliding through the waves with complete ease, like I was just skimming over the tips of the small waves magically hovering over them with the mountains getting closer.

As I got closer to the mountains, I noticed they were of the most pure, the brightest, most vibrant White Mountains I had ever seen in my life, and all I could think of was the white cliffs of Dover at the time I was heading towards them, but they looked nothing like the cliffs of Dover. They were much taller with no wear and tear from the beating of constant waves of the ocean; they were sparkling white and so pristine looking and a vision of perfect natural beauty.

I proceeded to head closer to the White Mountains and as I got closer, details started to appear on the rock face on the side of them. Suddenly I could begin to see a female face starting to take form and appear the face was so angelic, a face of pure peace and tranquillity.

It was a face of sheer comfort with a strong feeling of un-doubtable trust that was resonating with my whole being. The eyes of the most vibrant ocean blue as the rays of the Sun hit the mountain face, lighting it up and creating the most wondrous shimmer with a beautiful sparkle coming from both eyes, as if they were cut from the finest facet of Diamond imaginable.

Totally unaware to me my head had subsided backwards, I had become so relaxed my neck muscles stopped holding up my own head as I absorbed the energy, whilst seated on the chair. It was like I was having a full body massage that was being created purely by vibration and frequency. This frequency I am feeling from the universe is total unconditional love and I can feel the toxic emotions leaving my body, as they no longer serve my purpose, as it was my time to begin my healing process.

For the next few moments I was just floating in front of the face, and continuously looking straight at it. The face was looking back at me, with love, and a gentle smile, emanating from the 'mouth shaped' part of the mountains face. I suddenly started to hear a gentle voice "Spencer it's time to come back now." The healer gently said to me.

Eventually I did come back around, with the healer standing in front of me "Everything ok?" He softly said. Due to the level of deepness I went during the healing it did take me nearly a full 10 minutes to talk me back around, the healer told me "It's took me longer to bring you back, than the time I spent healing you." He explained, then went on to say "I removed my hands from your shoulders around 10 minutes ago, and I have been trying to call you back ever since."

By his reaction what had happened with me that day, clearly never happened with anybody else before. As a healer you are responsible for the intention you set prior to giving anybody healing, and you must always ask permission before you place your hands on anybody.

Remember the healing energy does not come from the healer, it's not his/her 'energy' I am receiving, but I am receiving the energy created by the universe because of the intention the healer has set. Whatever you are doing within your spiritual path, the intention you set tells yourself precisely what you are – for example, you are what you focus upon.

If the only focus on your spiritual path is to get rich, then that's your intention, that's your focus and unfortunately in times of now the 'Spiritual Movement' has become far too commercialised, and this will affect the way spirit will work with you.
The reason being is because in the universe money does not exist because it's man-made; it is not a natural occurrence of energy. The gentleman that gave me the healing had the most pure intention and

that is why I benefited from the healing, as there was an exchange of energy. I eventually came fully back around, feeling very different, much lighter, more relaxed and feeling much more positive. I then thanked the gentleman and got myself a cup of coffee, so I could tell Marie what happened, we found a place to sit, and began to talk quietly over what had just happened, Marie said "you were out for a while, they only gave around 10 minutes of healing." Marie continued "The woman had finished healing me, and I turned to look at you, and you looked like you fell asleep with your head back and your mouth open trying to catch flies" as she said quietly laughing to herself.

We finally left the church on a high note and headed back into the city centre to get a bite to eat, so we headed to one of our regular places we ate in if we went into town. The way I was feeling was much better than prior to going into the church for healing, I was so much calmer and had more clarity in my mind and a huge burden had been lifted off my shoulders.

There came a point with my spiritual development where I started to find an interest in giving healing to others and a lady I knew at the time called Joy was teaching Reiki, and was looking for students to teach level one as she had just qualified as a 'Reiki Master'.

Because we were her first set of students and we were Joy's guinea pigs let's say, a couple other friends, my mother and myself joined-in and we were taught level 1 and 2 Usui Reiki for free. Like everybody else, I followed the guidance from the Usui Reiki manual and getting a full understanding of the 'Do's and Don'ts' whilst being a Reiki level 2 practitioner.

At this point I opened a shop called 'The Little Shop Of Angels' of September 2005 in Holbrooks, Coventry (U.K) and this was a base at that time were I did numerous Reiki treatments. Through the help and guidance of those around me and spirit, I decided to set up a business and open a shop to provide them with the things they may need to help their spiritual journey.

The shop sold the usual various items such as; Crystals, angel, Fairy ornaments, Angel/Tarot and various books. Whilst I ran the shop it also allowed me to start teaching mediumship alongside Pauline for 3 years before teaching alone. I did private one to one readings from the room above the shop also.

Within this same private quiet room it gave me the opportunity to provide healing for those who wanted it. I was a sole trader with no paid staff, I had the amazing flawless help and support from my mum helping with the running of the shop when I was doing readings or healing, and if she wasn't available, a friend would step in and help at times.

During the period of time I was doing healings from the room above the shop, one particular occasion a young woman came in to my shop with her husband, and enquired about the healing treatments, as she had been involved in a car accident a couple of years prior which caused a knee and hip problem.

The particular lady had been through various medical treatments of physio and a combination of pain relief medication and she felt it was time to try an alternative therapy. We sat down and went through various things of how I worked at that time, what Reiki is etc etc. When I booked people of the opposite sex I always insisted to bring a person with them as a witness during the treatments, I did this for my own protection, and I felt it would make women feel more comfortable if they are not alone and had someone with them they knew.

The lady and her husband returned on the day scheduled for healing, and I asked how she was, the woman replied "I have been struggling the last few days, it's like that sometimes, the pain is up and down depending on what I have been doing." My mum was holding forte in the shop as the three of us went to the treatment room.

The woman laid down on the treatment bed face up then I covered her body, leaving the head clear with a purple blanket, I put on some gentle music that I used for meditations and healing. Whilst the woman was relaxing I sat for a couple of moments just to get myself mentally ready and composed setting my intentions, and also calling upon my healing guide to assist me as the healing comes through us, not from us.

Once I felt prepared I placed my hands gently over her affected knee the energy begins to draw in as my guide that works with healing comes forward and gently blends his energy with mine. At this point I am quite aware of what is going on around me, I could hear the music lightly playing in the background, and every once in a while I could hear the lady's husband moving in his chair.

I glanced over to the husband just as a gesture of acknowledgement and he was watching with great intrigue and interest of what I was doing. I closed my eyes and began to focus in myself again; the energy from my hands was a gentle cold feeling.

The energy from my guide was coming through the back of my head towards the lower base of my skull the frequency of healing travels down both arms into my hands out through my fingertips into the recipient.

As I continue the treatment I notice the lady's leg I was working on moved downwards sharply, I looked up to the lady to see if she was ok, and she was still in a very peaceful state and looked undisturbed, so I put it down to her moving to get more comfortable.

The healing treatment went on for around forty minutes or so, and when I felt the energy disperse I began to close down the healing session and gently call the lady back. I took a minute or two for the lady to open her eyes. I advised her to just rest for a few more minutes, this allows the human mind to fully come back to its full and natural awaken state of awareness.

The lady sat up and I gave her a glass of water as sometimes people can become thirsty after healing, also a fresh glass of water after healing, I find helps the body cleanse itself of other toxins. I asked how she felt and she replied "Yes, thank you that was lovely, and er... different." "Different?" I asked. The lady then asked if I had pulled her leg sharply during the healing as part of the treatment. "No, I am not qualified to do such a thing, performing such a task without the correct teaching or knowledge of what I was doing, could cause more harm than good." I went on to explain.

She replied "Oh, that's odd I wonder what that was?" my reply to her was "I thought you moved to get yourself more comfortable, also if I did sharply pull on your leg, your husband would of witnessed it as he was watching me the whole time." The husband did confirm "Spencer's hands were on your knee the whole time, he definitely didn't pull on your leg during the treatment." The lady felt ok now to get off the therapy bed so we all went down stairs into the shop, where they both said thank you and left.

Several days later the same young couple returned, as they entered the shop I welcomed them both with a friendly "Hello guys, how's things?" They walked up to the counter and the lady said "Do you remember the healing you gave me last week?" "Yes" I replied, "You are the lady that had an accident and came for healing on your knee and hip" I confirmed.
She started to smile that was followed by a sniggering laugh, "Well you are not going to believe this." She said sharpishly still with a giggle in her voice. "Before I came for the healing I was taking up to 7 different forms of pain killers including Morphine daily, and since the healing I have managed to reduce my dose to one dose of Morphine a day." She confessed.

"What? No way?" I said with a tone of shock coming from my voice. The husband then added "She is telling the truth, I don't know what happened, but her pain has reduced a lot." I was totally thrown with what they said, my mum overheard the conversation "That's amazing, what do you think is the reason Spence? My mother asked. At this point in my development I didn't know what fully happened, but what I said was "It must have something to do with your leg being tugged sharply; my guide must have pulled your hip in to alignment maybe?"

The lady went on to say "Well, whatever happened it's improved my movement due to less pain, thank you." "Don't thank me." I said "It's the universe that did that not me." The lady then replied "I am going to keep an eye on my pain levels, and if they increase, we shall return for another treatment, if that's ok?" "Yes of course it is." I confirmed.

I cannot give a full analysis of what happened nor can I confirm the lady's condition now, because this happened in 2007/2008 and the couple never returned. I can only presume either/or/ combination of the healing treatment adjusted the problem to a manageable pain level, or though further treatment of the medical world of specialists, I may just never know.

Over the years my healing has changed a lot, and so has my understanding of it, here is a recent healing experience I had with a friend I worked on who has various health problems including issues with her spine and neck, and she needs an aid of a crutch to walk around.

My Friend Pat has had healing from me over the years and has also had readings to. Pat is a mutual friend I met through Pauline who helped me develop my trance mediumship and Pat was in that particular home circle. Our agreement for exchange of energy was Pat received healing free of charge as she very kindly offers to drive me around.

This lady has helped me hugely over the years giving me lifts to church services around the country since the passing of my mum in 2011 as I don't currently drive because of my eyesight, and the healing treatments are a symbol of my appreciation and gratitude.

This healing treatment happened in November 2018 and was very different from previous experiences and the energy was very different. From the period of 2016 to 2018 I hadn't done much healing due to coming very close of being homeless myself and dealing with my own life lessons, and growing further in my own spiritual development and making changes within myself. This has included change in lifestyle habits and removing certain things out of my body such as little or no alcohol. No fizzy drinks no dilute drinks, no caffeine, no dairy, and no meat so I can be on a more high frequency, high vibrational organic fruit and veg diet, because everything we ingest affects our physical health and vibration of our physical and light body, but this will be discussed further in this chapter later.

Pat arrived a couple of minutes early so we had a brief catch up chat, and she also enquired about a trance reading on another day with my guide Chow Li. This is because I know a lot about Pat as we have spent quite a few hours on motorways together, whilst she has taken me to places of work. After a brief chat I got Pat to settle her mind and make herself comfortable prior to the healing session, whilst I set-up the music before I sit with my guide again for a few moments to clear my own mind.

I sat just for a few moments and called in my helper Mr Chan, or as now I can call him 'Chan'. This is the name he introduced himself as to a friend whilst I was giving her sister some healing to her knee around 15 years ago. When that friend who is also a medium asked his name, he replied "Mr Chan". That friend then went on to ask my guide "What's your first name?" to his response abruptly "Mr, to you." When I was told after that healing session we all had a good laugh about it.

Sorry for going slightly off track I felt I had to add that short paragraph of explanation, Chan is not so abrupt now and is quite a charming character.

During the healing treatment I had a YouTube video playing in the background which played an on-going sound wave of 432 Hz. The reason for this is because I am now aware listening to these different frequency sound waves, each one has a different effect on helping the body heal, some of these frequencies can also help DNA repair. This I didn't find out through Reiki development, I found this out through independently studying, researching how to heal the body and raising my conscious level of understanding through the having the guidance from my spirit team.

As I began the healing I noticed the energy was very different to what I was used to in the past, for many years I have worked with a cold energy around me when I work, but on this occasion the energy was much colder than that. As I was working with Pat spirit began assessing her condition to decide what to do in this particular treatment, I remember starting by placing my hands on her shoulders and the healing started from there.

A couple of minutes had passed and suddenly I felt, as what I can only describe as 3 'rods' of energy, that was working with me. One Rod of energy was flowing down my left side, pressed against the outside of my shoulder, and the same to my right hand side. I suddenly realised the two 'rods' of energy either side of me were holding me in place so I couldn't walk sideways; I had to stay standing directly behind Pat as I was passing on the healing, and I found this very peculiar as it had never happened before.

The third 'rod' of energy was travelling straight down through the top of my head and down my spine into the ground. Although I didn't see them as my eyes were closed but the energy rods felt very solid like and very rigid. The rods felt as if they were going from floor up to ceiling, almost like concrete pillars that one can see on various buildings.

The third rod of energy that was going through me stopped me from having the ability to move my back, head and neck as it was all locked into place, to form a feeling within myself as perfect posture. Whilst this was happening I can honestly say I didn't know what was happening, but I stayed completely calm as I knew it had something to do with the way the universe chose to work with me.

During the healing I could move my arms and hands that where guided round to be placed where needed. With using 3 fingers on my left hand that where being guided as they worked softly on various vertebrates in the neck and spine, and my right hand gently placed on her shoulder. During the healing I noticed Pat move about of which we both heard various gentle cracking sounds coming from her back as the energy aided her posture carefully. During the treatment I never instructed for Pat to move, in fact I never spoke to her at all during the healing, as I was too focused on what the energy was doing.

Once I had finished the healing, Pat confirmed that she felt spirit energy manipulating and realigning her back, only slightly and very gently, and also felt different temperatures of healing energy varying between hot and cold.

Like I have previously said I have never experienced anything like that before working with healing and spirit. At present up until writing and completing this book it hasn't happened since, so it will be interesting to know if, and when in the future this could happen again.

Below is a brief update on the healing to Pats back, some feedback, which I was given around 3 days later. I phoned Pat to double check about a lift arrangement.

She told me after the healing she felt slightly tender on her back and neck for a couple of days, but she said she had no pain in her back and neck. I asked how it has affected her mobility, she confirmed for 3 days she was able to move her head left and right much further than she could prior to the treatment.

Pat also spoke about the energy going down her spine; she described it as a very cold 'blowing' down her vertebrae of the spine internally, and around the neck. She said her right shoulder and arm still had some pain, but not like before. The relief of the pain was short lived and lasted around 5 or 6 days, Pat is still continuing to receive healings from me.

My understanding and view point of how I see healing work, has changed hugely with me now, than when I first started my journey working with healing energy and my guides over the last 17 years. After a couple of years of doing Reiki healing and doing things provided by the healing handbook has now become irreverent.

Many techniques we were taught from the manual (except hand positions on the body whilst healing) suddenly also became irrelevant to me, as I began to feel it was just 'Mans input' to jazz it up and my guides said all I have to do is sit with them and set intention for healing to be given.

I now understand that these habits we are taught to do prior to giving healing treatments, are nothing more than "Rituals" or 'Visual aids for the mind' as my spirit team puts it, and the hand symbols do not make you any more powerful or improve the healing you are providing. To generate 'power' is more complex behind the scenes than that, and the type of energy we pass through all depends on us.

Although the hand signals are not necessarily needed it is more of a visual tool for those beginning their healer practitioner journey to give them a 'focus' for 'creating' the intention or the starting process of the healing session to put the healer into the right frame of mind.

For many years' people came for various healing treatments and the more I worked with spirit, the more it changed over time; the reason being was because I just allowed myself to be guided by my spirit team. During my development in mediumship and healing, many a time I was told I should listen to the teacher over my spirit guides, ladies and gentleman that's a power trip and coming from the human ego.

In all the years I have been teaching mediumship I have always told my students learn to trust their guides, once they know the guides are working from a place unconditional love, and if you haven't tested your guides of their intentions, I suggest you do.

This is not a disrespectful act, you receive back from the universe from the energy and intentions you put out, your guides will reflect a true reflection of you, so you need to know what their intentions are, and you need to be clear and sure about your own. If they are not following natural law or coming from a place of truth and unconditional love, then you need to ask for a new spirit team. You can directly ask your helpers outright if they are following Truth and Natural Law and they must respond. The universe cannot lie, in fact energy and frequency cannot lie so if you don't get a response you will know otherwise.

It is absolutely paramount you work through the heart with total unconditional love whilst working with spirit, as we are constantly creating good and bad karma all the time through our words, thoughts and actions, hence it's vitally important how we speak, think and act.

My advice to anybody reading this book, please make sure your spirit team have the best intentions for you and humanity, it's your moral obligation. Also sit regular with your guides because you will find teachers come and go, and not all have the best intentions, but your spirit guides will ALWAYS have your back if YOUR intentions are pure.

Any conditions or lessons for the soul need to be taught, we have to learn and grow, and if we don't learn we repeat certain life cycles and situations due to not fully understanding why these situations happen. Building a rock solid relationship with your guides over time will help guide you in the right direction and although they guide us, it's always our choice to take their advice or guidance, or not as we all have free will.

I have learnt the human mind complicates everything we do when working with spirit, it breaks things down, and it amylases everything, instead the mind needs to be out the way and just allow the energy to flow through you. Whilst healing the energy that is given is not coming from you, it is passed through you, and yes you get a first 'dose' of the energy but our intention must only be set to give to others, and not to do things and expect a return.

This method is similar to the way you would prepare yourself if you were to do mediumship. The only difference is if you want to work with healing, you have to extend your energy further up to blend with the correct source, as it's not the intention of Clairvoyance you are setting to do, it's healing.

When I do healing my guide who works with me blends his energy with mine for assistance with each treatment I do. I am not going to put a label on him and say he is 'a doctor' this is nothing more than a 'Earth label' as he is simply a soul that transfers healing energy through me to the recipient, and he instructs and guides the movements of my hands during each treatment.

During healing with permission from the client, our hands are allowed to be placed around various areas of the body such as head, shoulders, and back for example. Remember though, whilst practising healing, healers must always ask permission to place their hands on people that has requested the treatment.

After couple of years I started to ask myself questions about the way we are taught about healing, because the more I observed and listened to the rules I was told, it became apparent all these ideologies we are fed, are just man-made limitations. For instance I remember at the beginning of my path we were told to never place our hands on the top of somebody's head over their crown chakra because it 'blocks' the flow of energy, I find this again another man-made rule or limitation.

Objects are energy and energy has been flowing through solid objects since time began and it's that same source of energy that has created everything. The only way we create blocks is by listening to the limitations of human mind and ego. To be a clear vessel for spirit the mind and the ego has to go, and only unconditional love should be present.

The reason I began to question everything about what I was taught, was because when I was sitting at home with my guides and meditating I was getting told a very different point of view. For 4 or 5 years I was following the same 'rituals' with 'charging' the energy, and opening the chakras in your hands with the Cho Ku REI symbol, but in all truth it is not required.

Do you believe when Jesus did healing he used these 'ritual' hand signals to get the healing energy from source? Of course he didn't, he used the knowledge from the source of Consciousness. Jesus knew setting his intention is the initiation of power, creating what it is you want to do.

Consciousness, universal energy, is completely limitless; it goes beyond all the physical limitations of what this 3D world has over us, the energy is working upon frequency and it is changing the light code within the physical, the energy and frequency provided by the universe works on many levels of the body, as it will work on the physical, emotional, mental and our spiritual bodies too. Dis-ease is caused through toxins that build up within the body, which is caused through many ways at how we live our life.

Over the past couple of years I have come to the realisation whatever we do and put into our bodies affects our frequency. Things such as positive and negative thoughts, day to day situations, our habits, our actions, how we treat others, our mood, drug use (legal and illegal) food and drink and so much more in our own lives have an effect on us. All the above also affects how we work with spirit and the energy we are using or what we are provided with from the universe.

The purer the vessel (body) the higher the vibration of frequency we use, because if we eat high vibe/ frequency food it ascends our point of awareness allowing us to use a purer form of universal energy coming from higher realms of consciousness from a place of unconditional love.
Whilst eating things like junk food and fizzy drinks such as cola regularly, and putting things into our bodies that suppresses our conscious point of awareness and dampens that energy, creating us to work with a lower level of consciousness, who have a lower point of awareness, and understanding than those that have an ascended soul/awareness.

The quality of energy we use during healing, and what it is capable of, is determined by many things, and diet is one of them, also what you believe to be true by what you have been told through man's ideas. Or what you resonate to knowing to be true, through expanding your point of awareness through ascension of your consciousness growth, by following the guidance and teachings of your guides and the universe.

During healing, our minds must be highly disciplined as the thoughts that come into our minds can alter the frequency-waves of healing, and also cause a distraction. Thoughts contain energy and the energy from those random unnecessary thoughts can transfer and absorb into the recipient who is receiving healing. If your thoughts are negative then you are passing on negative energy from those thoughts.

There are actually many factors that will affect the energy we use whilst giving healing, and one major factor that is ignored is our own energy, and that is something I understand more now on a much deeper level. During my Usui Reiki training the group had to do a '21 day clearing' this clearing is to remove old emotions, various blocks and more, and over the last few years on my spiritual path I have come to realise it isn't possible to 'clear' all the old baggage in such a short space of time.

To have cleared out all these old emotions and life blocks, and to become a 'cleaner' source of energy, we need to fully understand why situations have happened in our lives, we need to break old cycles and habits, and have an understanding of karma in our life. Before we can start truly healing ourselves we have to complete our souls' lessons, and you cannot do that in 21 days. This can take years or even your whole life time depending how we choose to think, act and live our lives.

From 2018 when I had any healing treatments booked in, I was told not to eat meat on that day, and I need to work on completely removing meat out of my diet. At this present time I still consume a small amount of meat in my diet, but this is one area in my life I still need to address, but thankfully I am improving.

I now know when I have no meat in my system and I am only eating or juicing fruit and veg the energy within me feels much better. I feel less tired, more energised and my mind is much clearer because I am eating high vibrational, high frequency organic food. When we eat meat and processed food it lowers our frequency and vibration within the body and this affects the energy we are using whilst working with spirit, and this was made aware to me in mid-2018.

Everything we eat and drink affects our energy and vibration of our body, and not just the physical, it also affects our light body too. Meat is something that lowers our frequency and consciousness, if you eat something that has been killed its 'dead' and therefore it contains no life force energy like fruits and vegetables do.

Meat is also acidic; our bodies should be alkaline and have a PH level of around 7. Alkalising the body can help prevent various illnesses, and health condition. For many years I was unaware of what we put in our bodies affects us the way it does, on so many different levels and throughout all my years of development, the large majority of mentors on my spiritual path didn't make me aware of how our diet affects our spiritual energy and clarity. The only advice I had was eating prior to working with spirit, because this avoids us from getting diabetes.

I do know through my spiritual development that this is true as my guides have confirmed this. When working with spirit it can and does have effects on us because if we are not putting the right food source/energy in, then the spirit world have less good energy to work with, thus causing various health problems, and I had confirmation of this around 6 years ago whilst I was teaching a development circle.

I didn't end up with diabetes because I always made sure I ate prior to working but I was getting an inflamed spleen due to not drinking enough water.
For weeks I was getting home after running the circle and at the time I was helping students develop their trance mediumship, and every time I got home I kept getting the same pain on my upper left side and I didn't know what it was, and this pain only came on after circle work.

I phoned a trusted mentor at that time and discussed it with them, and they said I needed to drink more water whilst working with spirit. I was told when sitting with spirit it can add extra stress or make certain organs work harder, therefore the drinking of water helps replenish lost energy, as water is good conductor of energy when we drink plenty of it.
Water also helps the energy flow around the body better, and flushes out any unwanted toxins and old energy out of us. Once I started increasing my water intake whilst working with spirit, the pain went very quickly and never returned.

I will admit at this present point in my life whilst writing this book I am still working on my own eating habits and lifestyles, and I have removed many things from my diet that does not serve my body well. I know old habits are hard to change believe me, there was times in my life I wouldn't think what was happening to my body when I was in a local chip shop ordering a large kebab.

I realise now they didn't do me any good, so I had to change my own eating habits. I know what I am writing sounds rather preachy, but I wish I knew then, and was told about what I am just coming into awareness of now, much sooner.

We have to keep working on the things that need to be changed to become more conscious of what we need to do in our lives to improve it. It is the only way change will happen and old cycles can be broken in order to make room for new and fresh cycles to manifest and improve our life and well-being for ourselves, and others.

To be a better vessel for healing we need to put the right foods into our system, our bodies work just like a car engine, if you put Diesel in a Petrol car it's not going to run to its full performance potential, and our bodies are exactly the same. If healers are ill themselves, then in my opinion we should work on our self, before we can go giving healing to others because if we are not feeling 100% then we cannot give our all.

Bear in mind when administering healing we are transferring energy knowingly and unknowingly that is within and around us, and we can pass that energy on. For example if you have an argument prior to giving healing, you have absorbed negative energy from that situation, and if you haven't released that prior to a treatment from yourself and the environment, you can pass that energy on and the recipient will feel it during the healing, and this then interferes with the treatment session.

Since 2015 I did some research in juicing fruit and veg after a friend mentioned it during training for my first half marathon so I looked into it and tried it. After looking into it I started to make homemade fruit and veg Smoothies on the days of doing a healing, and then meditate about an hour before to clear my mind and get myself ready.

Meditating raises the vibration frequency within our body, and also raises our consciousness, allowing us to blend and connect to higher sources of healing energy that is provided from the universal consciousness of unconditional love.

The energy, or light code provided when we address healing comes from the universe, and it is that light code correcting our frequency code. This is a very simple explanation of what is happening during healing, but it goes much deeper than that, and that is something I am still learning about along my own journey as I am researching more of the workings of our physical and light body.

As regards to healing with myself, it has been a continuous effort trying to improve my own wellbeing and working on areas in my own life that has allowed healing within me to happen. Healing self-starts with the way we think about ourselves and the way we think has an effect on how we deal with situations and people around us.

Throughout this book I have mentioned about my own eyes and not being able to drive in my past, when I was a toddler my eyesight was quite poor. As I got older, I was told by my mum and dad that they realised about my sight, when my dad was waving his car keys in front of me, and I apparently did not react. This raised some concerns, enough to gather an understanding if I was blind or deaf. I was told by my parents from an early age there were tests carried out on my eyes as a young child, and I had tests such as a wind tunnel test, and working with my sight with the use of wearing glasses, and putting a patch over the lens of my glasses, of my stronger left eye to strengthen my weaker right eye, and vice versa. This was done during the period of time in nursery and junior school, and I have never had any eye surgery.

My dad, bless him, did his upmost, just like my mum to help me improve my sight, so I could live as 'normal' a life as anybody else. Around 6 or 7 years old, I was playing at a friend's house across the road, and when it was time for me to go home, my dad would be waiting on one side of the road checking traffic, and I would be standing on the other side of the road, with my friend and his parent to assist me across the road. I could walk about and do things, but I didn't need a cane, but crossing the road and judging the speed of cars, or even seeing them coming from a distance was a challenge. While waiting, my father would hold up a hand with his fingers up to see if I could count them, to keep testing my sight, there were times I got it right, and there were times I didn't, and there would be other times my friend would try and tell me, but he would get a clip round the ear from his mother, and we would laugh, but she fully understood what my dad was doing, as they were close family friends. The weather and light conditions also affected me more then, than it does now, once the 'eye test' by dad was carried out, I would be then escorted cross the road, or my dad crossed over to get me.

During junior school I was taught to touch type alongside writing, and any reading material would have been enlarged. Throughout growing up, I took part in playing many sports to my best of my ability at the time.

During an eye test, around the age of 12, I was told I would never be able to drive as my eyes cannot read the 6/12 line, that is required to get a UK driving licence. This became a major hang up for me when I turned 17, because of course most of, or nearly all my friends were learning to drive, and at that time, there was no chance that I could. The reason being I couldn't read a registration plate from the correct distance, this is because I have a stigmatism, my left eye is my strongest eye, and my right eye, well... its getting much better, which, when I was much younger turned-in a lot more than it does now, and at that time I could only read a car plate from around 22 feet approx, but I have managed to at least double that distance now.

 Through what I had been told at that time, and without knowing I had accepted that fate as truth and in having that thought process, stopped my sight getting any better. As I got older there was progress where I could do lots of the same things that my friends did while I was growing up.
I played sport and games, I loved playing football with friends, I did trampolining for my school, and did martial arts for 7 years through my teens, and got my brown belt, but had to stop due to a knee injury. There were limitations as my reaction time would be slower with certain activities I did, because as things moved

too quick, chances are, I would either see last second, or not at all.

I was never the best at the sport I played, but I never let my sight get the better of me. If was told I couldn't do something, at times I would still try it within reason of my own safety.

When I was in my late 20s, I tried out various places for laser eye surgery. On my final attempt I went to Harley Street, it was confirmed to me at that time; it was not at all possible for laser treatment on my eyes as it would make me blind. For many people this would have been a massive blow, but after sitting with the specialist, and being told why, it only made me more determined, and confirmed only to me, to rely on the powers of the universe, so that's when I really pushed for my healing from the universe.

Throughout the years of my spiritual path I have had many healing sessions on my eyes over the last 20 years and it's through these healing treatments in the past that has helped my eyes improve, and even the turn-in of my right eye is far less noticeable.

I have received healing in the churches, Rieki from friends, and I have had psychic surgery on my eyes during my own meditations at home. At one point during a meditation I received healing from my guides and they injected 4 individual 'needles' into each eye, thankfully they use energy not metal needles. Of late focusing on my eye condition I have had progress with healing of my sight through working on them myself.

I understand now everything within this physical reality all starts from an energy level, and the way we think changes our reality. The way we think limits our point of awareness, and limits us as an individual person. We are a reflection of our conscious, or higher self, therefore if I keep telling myself I can't heal my eyes in order to drive, then I create that limitation within myself and the universe will express that as my 'present reality'.

However if I change the way I am constantly thinking and change what I am focusing on, I can change that reality within this lifetime, because everything begins on an energy, or cellular and an atomic level, and through positive thought, and dedicated focus, the atoms and cells within the body react, which creates the process of manifesting change in the present physical reality.

Like I've mentioned in chapter 4 'Visiting the spirit world', it explains those in the etherical realms don't have that same limitation as us here, as they can manifest what they want, need or desire, and that happens because those in spirit 'KNOW' it is true in that reality and dimension. When we are born into this 3D/4D world this is the school of learning, and we are able to bring that knowledge into our current point of awareness, and be given the chance to prove it.

How long for something to show signs of progression, change and the level of success are dependent on many factors such as how you look after your body because what we eat and digest can affect our frequency and or your personal beliefs, plus much more to what it is you are trying to heal. Personally as regards to my eyes I am only conscious of the changes in my vision for the past 9 years where there have been key improvements on the last 3 eye tests from 2010.

From that I could say for the first significant change to be present took 11 years to manifest from 1999 but I never had the understanding like I have now all those years ago. For many years at the beginning of my journey I wasn't aware about the importance of understanding energy. The way I think and my diet would have also had an affect whether I was conscious of it or not.

It has only been the past 2 years I have begun starting to really understand how different forms of energy affect us. The natural laws and the Quantum Mechanics of the Universe is, what it is, regardless if we understand it or not, or even believe if those laws apply to us or not. They do as Universal Law is binding, and we cannot change the laws of physics but through these laws we can create changes with things within and around ourselves through our thoughts. Thoughts are energy and it's those thoughts that can be manifested into our present physical reality.

During growing up I was told my eye condition is hereditary from my grandfather, on my mums side of the family, from my point of understanding, and awareness now, I no longer accept this as truth, as I know my eye condition is to do with the conditioning of my soul, not a 'passed down' eye problem, so I know I can change it, and have been changing it over the past 10 or so years.

In February 2019 the healing I have done on myself was by having to go back, and work on the memory where I couldn't see the set of keys, and change that memory to me seeing a set of new keys. Through advice with my guides and friends discussing how to correct my sight, I have had to go back into my past and heal that area within my inner child, and also delete that memory from my existence, and from the records of consciousness within the Akashic Records, because it no longer serves my purpose, along with many other areas in my life, I have worked on and healed.

Over the past many years I have managed to change my reality and improve my sight because everything starts on an energy and an atomic level, when applying positive thoughts and focus through the 'I am presence' you are giving what you are focusing on energy.

The way the universe works is with enough attention, visualisation and positive affirmations of what you want to manifest the universe reacts to the thoughts words and actions you put out and then it's expressed back to us through the laws of attraction and manifests and becomes present in our life. It's paramount during phases of manifesting you stay completely positive and focused and must be specific on what it is you want to work on, and avoid as much negativity from others as possible, it's not their reality that is being changed, IT'S YOURS, own it.

For example when meditating and drawing in the healing energy and I use phrases like "I am manifesting into my present reality now for healing my eyes for perfect vision." or "I am giving myself permission to let go of all blocks and fears in relation to the improvement of my sight, and I am letting go of all that no longer serves me in my present reality and I accept to receive fresh new energy into my present reality now."

There has been a lot more I have had to do in order for this to manifest me driving into my present reality, I have had to meditate daily for around one hour, to an hour-and-a-half, and visualise myself taking driving lesson, also visualising driving my own car. The "I AM" presence' healing and manifestation process has been on-going for the past 6 months of 2019, the reason for this is because until then I wasn't fully aware of the true power of thoughts.

In order for this to manifest I have to 'know' in my heart that what I am doing is truth, and I do. When I am saying the affirmations either out loud or in my mind to myself throughout the day I now instantly feel a rush of energy builds up within my tummy area this feeling then makes me take a very slow, deep inwardly breath through my nose.

As the energy draws upwards from my stomach into my heart it makes me exhale slowly, pushing out and expelling the energy, very much like a deep sigh with a feeling of peace that then comes around me. The feeling then gives the reassurance and the feeling of 'knowing' and from this you then focus on the how it feels, and within your mind you have to visualise it and experience all the positive feelings that comes with that experience.

During my sessions of self-healing over the past months I have been experiencing many different sensations when receiving the energy. A lot of the time it's a strong feeling of tingling and throbbing of the eyes, it isn't uncomfortable; it's more reassuring if anything. It's like a gentle massage on the eyes. I have also felt energy in my eyes moving in a circular motion. The energy in and around the left eye was going clockwise, and the right eye was going anticlockwise, creating a balancing Ying and Yang affect. At the end of each healing meditation unwanted energy is released out through the top of my head from the Crown Chakra and destroyed by the violet flame.

Since 2010 there has been recorded improvement of my eyes from my opticians up to this year. After a recent eye test, with my new glasses I am able to read the driving line (6/12) on the Snellen Vision test with my left eye, but I can't read the letters immediately, so there is some more work needed on my left eye. My right eye has also made some improvements and also needs a little more work on.

This is a huge positive from that eye test, compared to when I was 12, back then I was only able to read the 20/70-20/50 lines on the Snellen eye test chart, I hope you are able to see (no pun intended) the improvements made, and my opticians are baffled. I fully understand this process will run its own cause, and I know this will happen in due time, how fast it happens all depends on me and how much I am prepared to work on myself, and this is true for us all. I now have to wait for my new glasses to see how I get on and go from there. There will be an update of my healing on my eyes in my next book.

Chapter 9
Bring me
Sunshine

While I have been writing 'Expression of Consciousness' it has allowed me to come to many realisations within my own life and address many things to improve my own wellbeing in order to help myself to help others further. During the past 18 months I have been healing areas of my life, and this allowed me to set myself free from old habits and repetitive cycles, and just cut things out of my life that no longer serve my soul purpose, making room for more opportunities of further understanding for my own soul growth.

There is good reason for me to bring this past situation up now as I have been writing this book I have had to open up old wounds that I thought I had healed from. I am going to take you back to a moment of my past approximately 5 months before I began my spiritual path. A time where everything was going to change in my life, and at a time I knew nothing about the spirit world.

The day my best friend took his own life I was so lost, some days I was just 'existing' without existing, so to speak, the pain and heartache for a couple of years was awful and I learnt to hide behind a false smile from the age of 17. At the time I thought no one else can surely feel pain like this? Is this the real pain of the loss of someone close? Growing up until the day Paul left this world, I hadn't faced a loss before, like that, the affect on me of a friends' passing.

There was a time in this period of pain and blur I wanted to end it all myself, I allowed things to get on top of me without really talking to anybody, like I said I hid it well from many, but one or two of my friends knew I was struggling. There was one occasion I felt I couldn't carry on; I felt beat, no more strength, and just raging with anger inside.

The constant dwelling feeling of guilt because I couldn't help Paul, although I had no clue I was going to face the dreaded day of the news of his suicide, because he hid it so well, but that didn't matter. You become so caught up in an emotionally hard situation that takes over everything in your mind, and you can't see what is truly going on around you at the time.

I was at home watching a football match on TV downstairs and I took it upon myself to make my sudden exit out of this world, I thought enough was enough. I just calmly walked upstairs into my room where there was a cupboard full of various bottles of spirits Brandy, Rum, Vodka and a couple other bottles that were stored for home parties/ Christmas. I looked through the various alcoholic beverages and suddenly grabbed the nearest one to me of which was a brand new litre bottle of Vodka.

I remember saying to myself something like 'bye world' as I cracked the new cap on the bottle with a quick twist; I took one look at the bottle as if it was going to be the last thing I would see. I stretched out my arm holding the Vodka and looked at it again. I put the drink to my lips and remember just tasting it for a split moment and to be honest at that time I didn't even know if this idea of an exit was going to work.

I felt my arm tense as I was just about to tip the bottle upwards to down the entire contents in hope it would end everything and put me out of the pain I was in. As I went to 'chug' the Vodka, very suddenly there was the loudest most bellowing shout of 'NOOOO!!' from a males voice.

I remember rapidly pulling the bottle away from my mouth and ducked my head because the voice came from directly behind me, the room went completely silent for a moment, not even 10 seconds, I muttered "Who the f**k was that? As I suddenly stood upright to turn around to see who was standing behind me, I turned to look and no one was there.

I was the only person in the room, I was completely alone, my mum and step dad were downstairs and for some reason they never heard it. How on earth did they not hear that voice scream at me? I know what I heard and I heard it loud and clear. "NOOOO!!!" The total confusion that came over me completely side tracked me, and immediately put a stop to what I was going to do.

I remember turning and looking back at the bottle and suddenly coming to the realisation of what I was going to do. I suddenly realised all the pain I was feeling at that time would have been inflicted upon my own family members and friends, if I had gone through with my actions, if it were to end my life there and then.

I remember sitting on the end of my bed and thinking to myself a change is needed, this behaviour cannot continue, it must stop now and it's only up to me to make it happen. I began to 'pray' I guess. I started talking to myself in my head and asking if there is help 'out there' I need help to get me out of this emotional battle I was then letting win.

I must of said a ton of things as I was sitting there alone for at least 20 minutes, to half hour just going through thoughts and the motions of what just happened with the choice I made, and this odd experience I didn't understand of someone shouting at me, and yet I couldn't see who they were, and no one else heard the voice either.

For the next couple of months I tried to keep myself occupied with work and college and daily saying to myself something is going to change and I will get through this, and that's how and why I was eventually lead to a spiritualist church. The universe knew how to get me to go to a spiritualist church because of my contacts in my youth work job. My friend Marie, who I had started working with months prior, was the 'Earthly Guide' the spirit world gently influenced to put me on my path.

Your spiritual development doesn't just happen in circle, or in church, we are all 'placed' in real life 'tests' where we have to help somebody, and those same tests/situations are put there to help you to understand and heal from certain elements that are in conjunction to the progression of your soul. Those test situations come with good purpose too, and they are put on our path to also help accomplish personal life lessons that are relevant for the further fulfilment of growth of the soul.

For many years I felt guilty for not being able to prevent Paul's suicide, and at 17 years old within the first 2 years after Pauls passing, I intervened and prevented 3 attempted suicides, two of which tried to cut their wrists and another tried overdosing on tablets. You can be placed in these situations 'deliberately' because they are relevant for breaking old cycles although I wasn't aware of that at the time.

The first was a friend trying to cut their wrists with a blunt knife, the second person did, as I didn't see them do it, but I got an ambulance and the third tried to O.D in front of me in a house that I was at with a couple of friends I knew at the time. I was still 17 with no spirit guides at that point, but for some reason I knew the person wasn't going to go through with their threats, and I didn't actually know this person at all.

The person was ranting over the way her boyfriend was treating her, she was quite a few years older than me with 3 or 4 children. The woman put the tablets in her mouth and after a couple of seconds I pinched her nose shut with my finger and thumb, within around 30 seconds they spat the gooey white mixed texture of tablets all over me as they didn't swallow and kept the tablets in their mouth. Then I verbally laid into her for doing it in front of their children.

Looking back those situations, they were there to help me throughout my spiritual path. I have had to deal with many suicides over the years in my mediumship. Paul has helped me in that process, and through this bought me to an understanding that helped me heal with Pauls passing. Every situation has a purpose.

Those situations I had to face were to stop those 'suicide cycles' because I had seen the damage suicide can cause as I had a form of understanding of it through my own experiences. I can only say from my own experience, I chose to do what I did because I 'lost control' of my emotions in my life, and I am so grateful for still being here now. I can honestly say I am grateful for all the good, and bad that has happened in my life, because without any of the things that have happened, I wouldn't be sharing my experiences now in my aim to aid and help others.

The day I considered ending my life here was thankfully intervened with, by spirit, and it was the universe that stepped in to break the cycle of history repeating itself in my case, and the times I was in, the situations of others contemplating suicide, where I helped and stepped in, I broke those cycles.

January this history repeated itself as a school friend committed suicide, and as a result, it left my longest and most loyal friend in a bad way, after she heard the news. Over the space of 2 or 3 months, my friend began to really struggle about the loss of a mutual friend, and I had to be there for them for a few weeks helping and guiding them through their own inner battle, of not being able to cope with loss.

Spending around 4 or 5 hours with them 3 or 4 days a week, for around 2 months talking to her counselling her if you will. Thankfully my friend has known me since we were 10 years old, and has given me her support throughout my own battles, and watched me grow in my mediumship over the years.

Due to the friend being fully aware of how I was with my own battles of dealing with suicide, she knew I could completely relate to how she felt. Through many conversations it allowed us to come to many realisations, within her life, and why many things happened.

I was able to work with her, through meditations sitting at a trunk of a tree, my friend felt connected to and I worked with her there.

Through the assistance of my guides, and at times speaking directly to her through trance, sitting in the middle of a field being embraced by the sounds of birds singing, and feeling the beautiful elements of mother nature.

During this time I was helping my friend, it started to make me come to many realisations within my own path and in turn allowed me to also heal many of my old wounds. Through this time it allowed both of us to have ascension in consciousness which means it gave us both a whole new level of understanding for our individual soul development.

On one of the days we went to the place to meditate I felt it would be the final process of the healing for this situation for her. After my friend did a 20 minute meditation, I guided her through, she came back around completely free of burden, and could finally see her life had fallen into place, and that her own future is now manifesting beautifully through its own process. That evening my friend had a dream about the mutual friend who took their life, I was told the dream was very life like, and felt 'real'. She was pleased to be informed when I told her she had visited the spirit world through her dream state, and did personally meet our friend, who we both know now has healed well in the world of spirit.

Sometimes you will need someone there, who may not fully understand how hard the work we as mediums do at times, but someone is there, just to listen and support you. My mum did just that, in life and in general with everybody. From knowing my mum I know what it means when someone says "Angels walk amongst us."

My mum passed away 8th September 2011 from pneumonia after a long battle of fighting emphysema and also Osteo and Rheumatoid arthritis for around 10 years, and I was her living carer for around the last 18 months of her life. My mum was the biggest inspiration to me, she was a woman with a heart of gold and she always saw the good in everybody regardless of how bad they may have been.

She had the most caring nature and would help anybody who needed it and she had the greatest sense of humour and was very well loved by many. It's truthful to say at times even though I am the 'working medium' helping many people over the last 20 years, but I know she has left the biggest impact of the purest light in many more souls than I.
8 years after her transition people at the churches I have worked at over the years who knew her, still talk

about her and share many memories, and speak of how she always made people feel better after she spoke to them. My mum always made people smile or laugh not matter how bad their day was, the whole time she was fighting her own pains and eventually got to a point where she was fighting to breathe. Over time it made it more difficult for her to go to the churches with me and help with assisting me in the shop depending how she felt day to day.

In 2010 my mum got to see me when I got ordained as a minister, and watched me open and run my own spiritualist group, the Temple Of Angels from September that year. She sadly passed one year later.

Before I get to that point, my mum was my rock for my spiritual path, because she had a basic understanding and a knowing of spirit. She knew in her heart her father had made many visits to her, and she didn't care who she told if they didn't believe her it didn't matter, it was her truth and no one was going to take that away from her. I learnt a lot from her in that respect and if she knew something was right in her heart, she wouldn't budge, and neither do I.

Many would say I am much like her in some ways; she was caring and gentle but she wouldn't take any nonsense, even though she was 4ft. 9. When I started developing, apart from Marie there wasn't really anybody else to talk to about what I was learning in circles, unless I was at the churches, so I had many conversations with my mum about what I was learning. In 2005 when I opened my shop and started to teach, with the help of Pauline for 2 years, my mum sat in the circle and I helped develop the abilities she already had within her.

For many years due to my eyes at that time my mum drove me to most of the services I did or to churches to watch other mediums work, so it created a very strong bond, much stronger than we already had. At times it was good that my mum was there, because there comes a time where there will be a reading that you do, it will be so emotionally challenging, you will need someone to off load it to.

When my mum started to attend a spiritualist church in Coventry not far our home, she made a lot of friends in that group and when asked "What song shall we sing this week?" my mum would always say "Bring me Sunshine" and she did that. She did bring sunshine into many peoples' lives because she was such a loving and caring person and would be there for anybody.

There will come a time you will try and help someone that has been shocked to their core so badly from a loss, you have to be prepared it could bring you to tears, once they leave the sitting you did, or church service. I will never forget one of my first private readings I did when I started out working in 2005.

A young lady had made a booking for a one-to-one reading and I remember looking at her eyes, and I could instantly see her pain, I was completely unaware and unprepared for how it was going to affect me afterwards. I took the lady through to the living room, and she sat on one of the arm chairs, and I sat adjacent to her on another chair.

I always give a brief explanation of how I work with spirit, in the sense that the spirit world uses a combination of the 3 'Clairs'. Clairaudience, Clairvoyance and Clairsentience to bring through various forms of information and evidence that is provided to allow the reading to unfold.

I began to connect to a loved one that identified themselves as the woman's grandmother, and the link came through on a very gentle energy and approached this girls' heart with the most compassion and tender care. The spirit world are very aware of precisely what is going on, and what has gone on within all our lives, in fact more so than we are currently aware of our self. The point of awareness you are at now and how much you may understand about your own life is a very small percentage in comparison to the infinite knowing of the conscious universe.

Your loved ones from spirit have seen every tear you have shed, every smile you have placed upon your face, and they have seen you fall and they have seen you rise from the depths of darkness when you thought you have nothing left. The universe is all seeing and all knowing.

The lady's gran came forward and bought up a couple of memories of her childhood with her Nan, such as reading her bedtime stories at the weekend when she stopped over. Or the fun times of her grandmother taught her to sow, and make her favourite stew and dumplings. I noticed the connection was overly gentle than other readings I had done in the past.

There was a feeling the spirit world were holding something or someone back, although the girl was enjoying the moment shared with her Nan, but I knew within me she was waiting for someone else to come forward, someone much more recent.

I became aware of a new presence of an energy coming into my own energy field other than the original communication from the grandmother. This energy felt very much younger, a very young child in fact.

This little soul was very nervous to come forward, I began to feel a large amount of strong emotion come through with the link of this child, at first I was not sure how this child was connected but I knew they were waiting to come forward. I finished off talking about the memories and evidence about the gran and told the lady a child was present, the atmosphere instantly changed within the room. The emotion became even more intense, the lady's eyes filled with tears before I saw one fall down her face a drip off the curvature of the young woman's cheek, landing on the jeans of her knee.

She suddenly gasped and then "Oh God." She muttered with a quiver in her voice full of emotion, I could see her throat lock up as the lady had to swallow. In my mind I became aware of the words "Mummy it's me." I felt this little child was female; she came forward with an appearance of a four year old.

I repeated back to the young woman what I heard and told her I feel she is coming forward as four years old, but I know she passed much younger I explained to her. It became known to me, the child passed around the age of 2 from a form of cancer. The lady began crying, I could feel her pain ripple through my system, and I had to hold back my own emotions, as I had never been in this situation before my guide told me I need to gain control of my feelings as I am here to help her and if I get too emotional, then that won't be possible.

I took a large gulp and a deep breath, this all happened within a few moments where I composed myself in order to continue the reading. The girl placed some sensations upon my body as I began to give evidence of some of the symptoms she had before she died. I could feel a build-up of pressure within my head which gave me great discomfort, I described what I was feeling and that's where the cancer started, confirmed by the sitter.

I started to tell the lady about some items that were placed in the coffin with her daughter, and I described a small pink cuddly toy the girl carried everywhere and the mother pulled the toy out of her bag then said. "I brought it with me in hope she would mention it." The lady smiled for a split second as she stared at the toy, before she began to cry again.

As a medium regardless of all the information and evidence you can give, sometimes it never feels enough, there are moments where a person will sit in front of you, with a huge void in their life after a loss, and that makes you feel powerless. At this moment in my journey I realised we can't 'fix' anyone in a 30 minute reading, their wound can take a lifetime to heal.

What adds more pressure, you realise the words you may say can potentially make them worse if not handled correctly, or not too seriously. That's why development of mediumship should never be rushed, like I said earlier in the book, we are dealing with souls, and those souls need the right care and attention.

The child confirmed that she had been visiting her mum from spirit and was two years old the girl confirmed, the parents hadn't touched the room since her transition to spirit. It was mentioned to me about the last photo taken in the hospital, and the girl told her mum she knew it was on their fire place, as I said, that the lady suddenly shivered, as the child's energy moved towards her mother to comfort her. More information was shared, before I bought the reading to a close.

I remember as I closed the reading and her loved ones withdrew, the lady sat there for a few moments in total silence, and continued gazing at the pink toy, "If you need someone to talk to, no matter when it is please call me, and I will talk with you for as long as I need to. No charge." I said to the lady. In that moment I didn't know what else to do, "Thank you" she said as she put the toy back in her bag to get ready to leave.

When the lady left, my mum was in the kitchen, I was living with mum, at the time she asked "How was it?" I remember looking at my mum and I couldn't speak, my own mind was blown away from the level of hurt this lady was suffering. "It was horrible." I said, as I broke down and cried on the kitchen floor "Her soul is broken" I managed to say through the crying. "Who came through?" my mum asked.

"Her daughter, 2 years old died from cancer." I replied as I was sitting on the floor with my head in my hands "Oh God." My mum replied, and gave me a hug, I remember crying it out for a couple of minutes while my mum was comforting me, then I thought to myself I need to speak to spirit.

I went to my bedroom to sit with my native guide Running Dear, as he was working with me at that time. I closed my eyes, still rather emotional and my guide came close and I felt a cold energy on my left shoulder as if he gently placed his hand there. Still sobbing to myself I said "This hurts so bad, I can't help people if it makes me feel like this."

Now let me explain, all our guides will handle a situation like this the best way THEY know how, and that also depends on the needs of the medium too, where you are at, in your development, or the way that particular medium thinks.

Like I said before Running Deer is very strict and can be quite firm and harsh, and at times very blunt, you could say tough love. He is the only guide that talks to me with such firmness, and many would think he is 'telling me off' but not at all. When I met Running Dear during my development, and after I got to know him I said to him "Don't ever bulls**t me! You must tell me the truth." So that's why he doesn't beat around the bush so to speak.

At this point in my development, he was all for tough love, he is a lot calmer with me now over the last couple of years, but on this day he wasn't pulling any punches. He was at first very calm softly spoken and started with "I understand why you feel this way, but you are right this isn't good for you, taking on this emotion from the reading, you must learn to instantly let it go." He continued "There is going to come a time where people are going to be in a real bad place emotionally, and you have to be strong enough to help them the best way you can."

"Yes it is very sad that the child passed with cancer, but that's the harsh reality of your world. That's what happens." He said to me a little firmer. "Holding back and controlling your emotions doesn't mean you don't care, or lack empathy, it means you are in control, and through that control, you will gain strength to face these hard situations." He added. "Very true" I managed to say, as I start to feel a little calmer and wiped my eyes.

"As you develop you will gain strength and learn how to deal with these difficult times, and you are going to have to prepare yourself for the worst." There was much more Running Dear and I discussed, but after around 15 minutes of us talking, I began to feel a lot better, and truly started to realise the mountain ahead.

The hard reality is sometimes you are going to have to face the not so nice things in this world because not everybody's path is rainbows and unicorns. I am not going to go into details in these areas, but I am sure you are aware at times life is not as pretty for some.

The most recent challenging of reading I did, was around 3 years ago, about a young man that got murdered but I cannot publish any of that information because the sitting was the most shockingly graphic reading I have had to do. I had to see and hear things I wouldn't want anybody to go through, and experience the awful final moments of someone's life and put it across to the parents of the person who was murdered, and believe me it's not easy, its heart breaking.

Over the past 20 years I have learnt that being a medium is something that comes with a huge responsibility, at first the universe guides you very gently and intelligently through your journey, and over time, things you are faced with, become more challenging. Now I have come to the realisation every situation is a lesson in life, and is a step closer to further understanding towards the overall enlightenment of truth, and without challenging times we simply would never learn, or expand our point of awareness of 'knowing'.

At the beginning of your path of mediumship everything you receive is in the size of small pieces of simplified information. Each single piece is an individual microscopic facet of an experience, of what you are truly capable of, in the future, if dedication and perseverance is your focus.

There are going to be times when the universe will make you cry in sheer overwhelming blissfulness, and there are times when the universe will bring you to your knees, break you, humble you, and through total unconditional love, it WILL rebuild you if you want it to.

Before I came on to my spiritual path, I had to experience loss and pain for myself, in order to give me a better understanding of grief, so I could help others. As a medium I have seen what a loss of a love one does to people, and over time I have come to the understanding we are all affected by grief very differently.

During your time of development you will find your own mind, self-doubt, and the human ego, on certain days, will be your worst enemy or your best friend, but if you build trust with spirit and your guides, they will carry you on the days that you cannot stand. They will be your strength when you are weak, and they will be your light when you are in your darkest moments of despair knowingly or unknowingly....

I was starting this new spiritual journey thinking it was only going to help me and nothing more. My initial intention was to self heal, I had no clue of what was to come over the next 20 years, and the kind of road I was about to take, the further lessons that needed to be learnt, and some of the hardest and most beautiful experiences with spirit that I was ever going to face.

At the time I had lost a best friend, but not knowingly I still had one best friend that had not gone anywhere, and that was my mum. Looking back now I can see how important my mums' brief insight into spiritualism was going to have on me. You see my mum didn't develop her abilities while we were all children growing up, so she was never able to advise me on how to improve my stills, because she didn't fully understand her own. Her moments, were at times, just very sudden and random when my mum experienced anything.

After the first 3 or 4 years of development I opened a shop which gave me the chance to begin teaching under the wing of Pauline, my mum then began sitting in my development circle I was running with Polly. My students really took a shine to my mum, and eventually they started calling her 'mum' like a lot of my friends did.

My mother definitely brought humour to the group because she was well known for saying the wrong words at the perfect time. For instance she is the only woman I know, that phoned her doctors to say "This is Mrs ...... I am just checking my appointment for my vasectomy." As you can imagine the line went dead for around 2 minutes, and I could hear my mum saying "Hello, hello, are you still there?" The receptionist responded with laughter "Yes Mrs... you have just made our day at the office."

My mum was totally oblivious what she just said, I am also laughing quietly to myself at this point, the receptionist then replied "Do you mean hysterectomy?" "Yes that's what I said didn't I?" so you now kind of get where I am going here...

In some ways it was a blessing she never did the platform, because when she was on the earth, my mum always got people's names wrong or said the wrong word. For instance when I was with her in B'n'Q and she got her words muddled up while asking for a dado rail, the word she chose instantly turned the face of the young lad to the same shade of red as the pile of tins of paint to the side of me.

She may have come out with the wrong words or names regularly but my mum was someone that would go to the person in the room that was alone and engage with them and make them instantly feel part of the group where ever she was. My mother did do her bit for a local church that is now called the Butterfly Group, she went there for many years at their old location and did chairing, and helped with some of the running of the group.

My mum did get to see me become an ordained minister in 2010 with the C.C.H.A (Corinthian Church Healing Association) through an independent spiritualist group I served many times. Like I said I am not religious, but the position served a good purpose on a few occasions.

I had a phone call once from a young woman saying she was having 'contact with spirit' I was told many things where going on in her home, but I knew something wasn't being told to me. I arranged to meet this person, and I was told by spirit not to go alone. I went with a friend I had worked with for many years, on platform together, and on our arrival we instantly knew something was very wrong.

The front door was wide open rubbish piled high outside, and the house inside was not in much of a better position either. As we approached the front door, I shouted "Hello" I then hear "I am in the kitchen." Gordon and I walked in to find a young lady standing next to the cooker with two hobs on keeping her warm whilst muttering to herself.

Gordon stood at the doorway of the kitchen and I walked in to talk to her "Are you ok?" I asked. She then said "Can you help me? They won't stop talking to me. I knew instantly this was a matter of mental health, and this is why addressing 'my self' as a minister, rather than a 'medium' was more suited.

As Gordon made a phone call to someone he knows working for social services outside, we kept each other in sight, as we were unsure of our safety. We found out this person was under the care of the Local Health Service, but had stopped taking her medication. I then had to phone various departments to find out who was the support worker for this woman, and notifying them why I was there, telling them I was a minister seemed a much better option than telling them I was a medium.

I am very glad I was placed in this situation, as this person was in a very vulnerable position, and thankfully I very quickly worked out this was a mental health matter, and not a 'spiritual' matter. When I made the phone call, I never mentioned I was a medium, Gordon and I felt that would have been a very bad idea.

During the time as a minister, I held two funeral services and one of them I had to do, was my very close school friend Craig, who was killed by a speeding driver when crossing the road at a crossing. When I got to his funeral, I met some friends I hadn't seen for a while, and yeah I got a bit of a ribbing from them, but it did lighten the mood for a moment, while we all shared a joke.

I then could hear my name being called out "SPENCER DAVID... SPENCER DAVID" I thought at the time they needed another person to carry Craig's' coffin into the chapel, but no Craig had somehow got the last laugh and one of the funeral bearers informed me there wasn't a minister organised and asked if I could do the service. I agreed to do it and thanks to my spirit team they gave me the right energy and comfort to do it, if I was meant to be a 'minister' just for those two moments in my life then that's fine by me.

I was eventually appointed Vice chairman for central in England for the C.C.H.A and worked alongside a great team and a great friend Dennis Binks for many years, until I felt it was time for me to resign my post in 2017.

My mum was my rock and managed to show her support in my first year in running my own centre;

The Temple of Angels, where I ran a development circle, which then lead towards a trance mediumship group. The centre held weekly clairvoyant evenings and regular development workshops throughout the year also.

It was practically a year to the day of opening my centre, my mum made her transition into spirit. I lived with her until she passed in 2011 after battling many years with arthritis and emphysema, after having a triple heart bypass in 2000/1. Being her live-in carer for around the last 18 months where her health deteriorated due to resulting in needing oxygen at home because of the emphysema, finally resulting in passing from pneumonia.

My mum was on 22 tablets a day to 'improve' her health, THAT IS 8,030 TABLETS A YEAR!!!! You would think being given that much 'medicine' she should have been cured.....
She had tablets such as Statins, Steroids, Anti inflammatories, pain killers you name it. At one point she was on so much pain relief her medication temporarily damaged her stomach lining. Throughout the whole time my mother was medicated for her health, it never improved, but for every symptom she had, the medical world had a tablet for that. From what I have witnessed over the years big pharma are nothing more than big business, they are only interested in profits, never the cures. That's my truth, and that's how I see it, and not just with my own mother either, I see it every day looking at everybody else around me.

It was decided to get mum more support in the mornings, so we had arranged with my mum agreeing for a nurse come in and help. On the first morning of this arrangement, for the nurse to come round, my mum was saying to me, she felt quite weak and her breathing was not the same, and that morning she was really struggling for breath.

The nurse arrived around 9.30am and I let her in and she did some checks on my mother. Due to the limited equipment the nurse came with, she needed a second opinion, and called for an ambulance, as the nurse was concerned, and felt something wasn't right. I informed the family, and went with her to the hospital.

When arriving at the hospital, I was met by my eldest sister Michelle. It wasn't the most pleasant hour or so I was there watching helplessly my own mother screaming in agony as the doctors are trying to get a needle into an artery in her arm to check her oxygen levels in her blood. It was difficult for the doctors because my mum had a very small body frame, and the doctors had to use child needles on her. After some tests and scans we got confirmation it was pneumonia, and she was settled in a room to herself.
Once my mum was settled and I had been with her most of the day I decided for other members of the family to see her that night and I would see her in the morning. The last thing I told her that day was "I love you, see you tomorrow." I went back to my girlfriends' house because it was much closer to the hospital and she also had an MRI scan the following morning.

The next morning I was getting ready to go to the hospital for my girlfriends' MRI scan on her hand and we decided we would go and see my mum after the appointment. As I was in the bathroom I was handed my phone as it was ringing, it was the hospital. I was informed my mums' health deteriorated over night and the hospital suggested getting the family there as soon as possible.

I got myself ready, and as I was waiting for a lift outside, Running Deer suddenly came close and began to talk to me. Like I have said previously he is blunt, truthful and straight to the point with me in our private conversations and he dilutes nothing. I said to him in my mind "You need to keep her here until I can get to the hospital and sort this." To his response "I am sorry you are going to have to close the church Tuesday." "What? Why?" I asked. "Your mum is with me in the spirit world." He completely engulfed me with his energy as he said it. "NO! That's bullsh*t! I am going to the hospital to F*cking heal her!" I addressed firmly in my mind and got angry with him.

"I am sorry that will not be possible, she is with me now and she is healed of all her discomforts. I wouldn't ever lie to you, especially over such a thing like this." I continued to block out what Running Deer was saying and insisting he must be wrong. Of course I am in total denial, and as I looked to my right to see if my lift was close, another presence drew near. Suddenly I could see a shade forming about two feet away from me, and as I began to concentrate Running Deer goes silent.

At first the presence wasn't very clear with no details, but they were short in height. I began to concentrate and focus on what I was looking at. It began to start looking like my mother, as features started to appear, as I am standing in the middle of the street. I could see her clearly but my human mind was having none of it, in my mind I kept saying "No, no, no, no, no, this can't be true." then the presence disappeared.

I then began to get very frustrated waiting for the lift, and like all of us do when things don't go right, we 'kick off' with the universe. "I need to get to the hospital NOW!" I am screaming in my head as I am frantically trying to figure out how to get to the hospital quicker. Then I see a bus approach the lights. I ran to the bus stop where I got on the bus with my girlfriend Kerry, I didn't say anything at the time of what had just happened, because I was still in denial.

The driver who coincidentally was someone I knew well said "Alright Spence?" I replied "No. My mum is seriously ill in hospital I need to get there ASAP." To his reply "Ok sit down I'll get you there as quick as possible."

He got me there quick alright; he deliberately missed the remaining 8 to 10 stops on route to rush me to the hospital, the universe works in weird ways. I remember as we sat down and were on our way an elderly lady behind me quietly said to who she was with "Look at that he is trying to get his friend to the hospital so he can see his mother." I couldn't speak I just looked at her and smiled. She looked back at me and I could see in her eyes, she knew what my fate was going to be when I got there.

I got to the hospital and located where my mum was and as I walked in the room, my 2 sisters and other members of the family were already there.

"Mum." I suddenly said abruptly as I entered. "You are too late Spence." My eldest sister said to me. "What?" I replied. "She passed about 10 minutes ago, you are too late." My sister confirmed. The realisation was so overwhelming I broke down and cried, my sister hugged me and we just cried together. It then quickly dawned on me I did see my mum in the street prior getting to the hospital and every word Running Deer said was total truth.

I remember standing at the side of the bed and looking at my mum, she was so peaceful looking, no more gasping for breath, no more physical pain and healed of all discomfort. "She is with Angel Michael now." I managed to verbalise from my mouth, the comment lightened the mood for a moment and we all had a chuckle through our tears.

My mum liked using the Archangel Michael cards and was always talking about Archangel Michael and she used to say things like "Oh he is gorgeous." or "I wouldn't mind him whisking me away." And would laugh to herself, so this was a common joke with many including those she knew at the church.

I sat on the bed to the right hand side of my mum and very quickly felt damp, I leapt up and brushed my hand down the side of my jeans "Err, I'm all wet." I said, "Oh that will be mums fluid coming from her body." Someone said. "Great, that will give mum something to laugh about." I said. This again lightened the mood for just a moment.

I then had to leave the room to inform my girlfriend Kerry at the time. As I walked out and made my way down the corridor I saw Kerry walking towards me "She's gone." I shouted as I began crying again. "What?" Kerry replies with a very shocked look. Kerry grabs me "She's dead!" I said as I began to break down again

After a few minutes I try pulling myself together to take Kerry into see my mum "Watch what happens now your mum is in spirit, she is going to let everyone know she is there." Kerry said. That did make me laugh and then made me think back to when I was waiting roadside for my lift and I saw her with me.

Kerry and I went into the room to see my mum; the other family members left us alone for a few minutes with her. Kerry and I started talking about my mum now being in spirit, and of course Angel Michael came back up in the topic again. As we were talking the room suddenly started to go cold from behind us, the temperature dropped very quickly and no doors or windows were open.

"She is here." I said "The room is freezing that's got to be her." I stated. After spending some time with my mum Kerry had to go for her MRI scan on her hand, as she had hurt it a couple of weeks prior. I spent time in the room with family sharing memories and just trying to think of good times to cushion the shocking blow for us all.

I joined Kerry after her MRI scan "How did it go?" I asked her, to her reply "It took bloody ages the MRI machine kept turning off." "The nurse said it has been working fine this morning until I got in there." I replied "What happened?" "Every time I put my hand into the machine it kept turning off, it happened three times." Kerry explained.

We both started talking and felt it could have something to do with my mum. As you can imagine it was a manic day and full of high emotion. We all took a duty to phone certain people to inform them of the sad news that my mum had passed. I phoned her brother William and passed on the devastating news, each time I phoned someone it got harder. Repeating the same information and getting the same saddened reaction became draining.

By the time I got back to Kerry's home in the afternoon, I was then receiving endless texts and calls from people that had 'weird' things going on in their home since the news of my mum passing. One phone call that day I received, I was told by the person on the phone they saw my mum appear to them in their living room. Many other messages were about light bulbs blowing and people felt that was my mum 'letting them know she is fine, that day there must have been a huge increase in light bulb sales because that's all I was hearing "I think your mum is here the light bulbs have blown in our living room." It was becoming very clear my mum was communicating from the moment she got to spirit.

My experience confirms our loved ones can instantly come back and communicate with us from spirit within a moment of passing. It's a very bad misconception that people have to 'wait' 6 months to receive a contact from a loved one that's completely untrue. If they feel it's time to connect immediately, they will. I was the first most likely person my mother made contact with that morning from spirit, because she knew I was the only one that would see her, and of course, to let me know she is ok where she is.

I have to admit, if it wasn't for my 10 years as a developing medium, and my belief and knowing that the spirit world exists, this is the only reason that I've kept my sanity. I am not saying my passing of my mum was easy, of course not. It did do one thing though, when she passed, it confirmed all my beliefs to be true, even though I was working with spirit for

10 years, and doing readings, and continuously communicating with spirit, but when your own mum dies it does something to you I cannot explain.

The day my mum passed I had something that others in the family didn't have, and thankfully that was my connection to my mum in spirit. Through this, knowing her spirit and soul is in a place of total love and peace brings me comfort, and her regular contact made it more bearable for me to cope with.

I have had the greatest blessing to see my mum come through during transfiguration, where her face appeared over one of the faces of my students in my trance circle that I ran, and I had a conversation with her. My father passed in April 2014 and I have also had the same experience, about a year after he passed and I also had a conversation with him.
The reason this was possible, was because the 2 students on separate occasions went into trance, and they bought them both through. The students were unaware of who they connected to, until after they came back to their own full awareness, and it is these experiences that have kept it together for me.

I have had many messages from my mum over the years from many mediums, the great thing is when my mum was here, she was never short of anything to say, and she still doesn't. (He He). My mum has played a major role with me from spirit, because when I have run Mediumship Workshops in the past, she has assisted my teaching by being a valuable communicator to help students with their development.

My mum, and Paul have helped with this too during the workshops, I split the students into small groups and inform the students of that group that they will communicate either with my mum or Paul, and provide the relevant evidence to support that. This has proved successful on many occasions, as both of them have helped my students build confidence in their development, and I have learnt from this our loved ones in spirit are not just there to help us alone, but because they are with the 'Oneness' of everything they can provide much more to humanity than just using them for 'self'.

The way my mum and Paul have helped in my circles and groups has helped me tremendously over the years, to heal from their physical loss, and that's the hardest part. There are certain days of the year I find it harder, like on their birthdays, anniversaries and Christmas, but I recently decided to look at those days in a different light, and bring a more positive approach to them.

When it comes up to my mums birthday, I can feel my mood change a couple of days before, leading up to her birthday on June 12, so this year I decided to change that and started writing the final chapter of this book, and heal myself further by writing about her.

Over the years, the more comfort I have had from receiving messages from my loved ones in spirit has given me the urge to understand mediumship even more, so I can carry that similar comfort to others by doing the same with my work.

Many people go into spiritual development with very little or no knowledge and understanding of it at all, just like myself. At the beginning it's all fun and giggles at times, because we are not aware of the full responsibility that comes with it, and a large percentage of your journey is to heal and work on your self, like my own situation with Paul, and then with my mum. Even though you may see it as you are only helping others. Whilst you help others, you are helping yourself heal and grow simultaneously.

Very few people if any will step into a spiritualist church and sit in a circle and suddenly think I am going to become one of those platform mediums. We go in quite blind and naive about it all, and of course that's not anybody's fault, you cannot go into a completely fresh and new experience or situation full of the right knowledge if you are not aware of what it is you need.

At the beginning it is very daunting, watching others pass on messages, and get all different kinds of information for others, whilst you sit there in silence. As you grow with your development, you will realise in those times you are still and silent, that is when the universe are working on you behind the scenes, that will allow you to do all those things soon enough.

In the moments of stillness it is when the universe is working on your light body, setting up and tuning the mechanics within you, and ascending your consciousness, helping with raising your vibration within the physical body, in order for you to communicate with those in spirit. There is no set time of how fast someone will develop, it's completely an individual's journey, and our personal growth purely depends solely on our own personal attitude, and effort we put in.

I have heard over the years "Oh you can meditate your whole life away if you want to; it's not going to make you a better medium." In fact I have learnt over the last 20 years the very opposite, meditation is one of the most paramount parts of your development and it will not only improve your mediumship, it will improve yourself as a person, and help towards your overall health and it does have many other health benefits. Any one of us can be a better medium, with the right development, but many of us don't develop being a much better person.

With meditation, sit alternating days meaning one day sit, and set the intention to only sit in the silence of your own energy (no spirit/ guide contact). This allows you to become aware of your own energy which over time makes it easy to feel 'new energy coming into your presence.

On the other, day sit with spirit and your guides, this will create a much better blend with your helpers, and bring in a much sharper connection with spirit. Sitting with spirit alone is completely safe, you set a loving intention to connect to spirit, and they will bring love back to you.

Sitting regularly with spirit, and your spirit team will help you raise your conscious awareness, the more questions you put to the universe, the better. This shows you are looking and searching for new knowledge and truth, and with the more truth you find out, the more you understand about who and what you are.

If you are starting out, sit for around 15 minutes daily and then build it up over a couple of weeks to about 30 minutes. Over the time of your development you can sit longer, once the mind is more disciplined, your mediumship development shouldn't be complicated;

we are the ones that make it complicated for ourselves.

You must ascend beyond thoughts, and the processes of the human mind concept, which creates limitations upon your journey. When you raise your consciousness, through thoughts and intentions of self we can project our point of awareness to higher dimensions, and work with guides from a higher level of understanding with a further clarity of truth.

You are a multidimensional conscious being. Your consciousness is completely limitless and it is constantly evolving, learning, understanding, and most of all continuously ascending.

Allow yourself to open your mind, and tap into that universal consciousness, that you are continuously connected to, and yes you are connected to this network of eternal frequency, regardless of the fact that you are aware or not. All we need do is sit within the peace and quiet, still our minds, and go within because that is where all our truths are held.

A lot of knowledge you need is already stored within your soul, there is not a spiritual teacher that cannot teach you, what your soul already knows. What those teachers do through their guidance is awaken your consciousness, so you can find your light, knowledge and truth within you.
Those that teach you should make you feel empowered, inspired, enlightened and humbled. They should speak with love and compassion, from their heart, and carry integrity and grace without the need to fuel their own ego, and want to push you to your fullest potential.

During your development you should be pushed out of your comfort zone, never look at spirit as stupid or inferior to you, constantly remember they are always many steps ahead of all of us, they know ALL our thoughts, feelings and actions. Embrace every moment with each footprint you leave within the sand, every experience is an opportunity of greatness. Each day is a chance to grow in knowledge and wisdom, don't waste a second.

You are the master of your own manifestations of the reality you choose to live within, allow yourself to focus on total enlightenment and truth, and raise your consciousness to higher levels of conscious understanding and higher dimensions, to connect to the Elders of knowledge and truth. The world is your oyster, you are in charge of your own future, you bare the gift of consciousness that gives you the power to manifest and create the path you crave to walk.

Your path is like the most beautiful Tree waiting to take full bloom. Your journey cannot be rushed, your soul is your seed. Knowledge and time is the watering of nourishment that your seed needs for growth. Your experiences are the leaves of your phases of growth, that are all part of your infinite make up of grasping further awareness of truth. Old unwanted leaves will fall, and these fallen leaves are to make room for new experiences, new understanding for growth of things that serve our true purpose.

Don't be enslaved by negative thoughts, these thoughts will lower your vibrational frequency, which affects your reality, and can create more negativity on your path, and dis-ease. There is more to each and every one of us than just existing within this physical world, there is more to life than just repetitive behaviour and living without true freedom.

You deserve much more than you have now, and all changes on our pathway begins within our self.....